TOMOCHICHI AND HIS NEPHEW TOONAHOWI

From a mezzotint by John Faber after a portrait by William Verelst. *Courtesy of Smithsonian Institution National Antropological Archives, Bureau of American Ethnology Collection.*

TOMOCHICHI

Indian Friend of the Georgia Colony

By

HELEN TODD

ATLANTA

CHEROKEE PUBLISHING COMPANY

Copyright © 1977

By Helen Todd

Todd, Helen, 1908-
    Tomochichi Indian friend of the Georgia Colony / by Helen Todd. — Atlanta : Cherokee Pub. Co., 1977.

    xiii, 182 p. : ill. ; 19 cm.

    Bibliography: p. 167-176.
    Includes index.
    ISBN 0-87797-040-8 : $7.95

    1. Tomo-chi-chi, d. 1739. 2. Yamassee Indians—Biography. 3. Creek Indians—History. 4. Georgia—History—Colonial period, ca. 1600-1775. 5. Oglethorpe, James Edward, 1696-1785. I. Title.

E99.Y22T657	970'.004'97	77-75268
	₁B₁	MARC

Library of Congress   78₁r79₁rev

ISBN: 0-87797-317-2

PRINTED IN THE UNITED STATES OF AMERICA

 Cherokee Publishing Company
P O Box 1730, Marietta, GA 30061

To
My Patient, Understanding Husband
Seldon Page Todd

CONTENTS

ACKNOWLEDGEMENTS

In my years as a junior high school librarian in Savannah I was asked frequently for data on the Indian chieftain Tomochichi. Dismayed that so little was available to satisfy the interest and curiosity of my pupils, I set about learning as much as possible about the great Mico who had been the friend of Georgia's Founder.

My quest for information has led me far afield, and in the process I have received assistance and encouragement from everyone whom I approached. I thank each person who made a contribution to the success of my effort, but especially do I express my sincere appreciation to J. Allen Spivey, Librarian, Clara W. Gould Memorial Library, Brunswick Junior College; Elizabeth Alexander, Librarian, Younge Library of Florida History, Gainesville; Bernard Berg, Park Technician, Ocmulgee National Monument, Ruth Trice, Archivist, South

Carolina Department of Archives and History, Columbia; Jan Buvinger, Reference Department, Charleston County Library; Edward N. Johnson, Chief, Bureau of Archives and Records Management, Florida State Department, Tallahassee; Norma Jean Lodico, Reference Librarian, U. S. Department of Interior, Washington, D.C.; the Library of Congress; James R. Glenn, Archivist, National Museum of Natural History, Smithsonian Institution, Washington, D.C.; Lilla Hawes and Marian Brown, Georgia Historical Society, and Cecile Richman and her Reference staff, Savannah Public Library; and to William B. Williford, president of Cherokee Publishing Company, who advised and assisted in organizing the material.

HELEN TODD

Savannah, Georgia
28 February 1977

ILLUSTRATIONS

TOMOCHICHI

1

TOMOCHICHI'S PEOPLE

An Indian boy was born about 1650 on the west bank of the Chattahoochee River[1] almost directly across from the present site of Columbus, Georgia. Nearly ninety years later this same child, by then the powerful and respected Mico Tomochichi, was to play a an important role in American history because of his support of the English in their efforts to colonize what is now Georgia. Very little is known about the life of this great Indian before he met James Oglethorpe on the Savannah River in 1733.

It is practically impossible to trace Indian genealogy. A girl was called by family terms or named after some natural occurrence or object connected with her birth. A boy was known as *ticibane*—"little boy" until he was initiated into manhood and given a name chosen because of achievement or a special trait. He was not permitted to intermarry in his own tribe but must choose a person of another group. Sometimes a member of one ruling family would marry into another reigning group in order to unite two family units or to bind an alliance. The baby inherited his mother's tribal affiliation. When the chief or mico died, he was succeeded by his next of kin on his mother's side, usually his nephew. The Southern Indians had no written language to record their history, so they recited tales and legends from generation to generation or pantomimed them in tribal dances.

The Indian civilization of the middle Mississippi Region had developed and expanded more rapidly than any in North America[2] except that of the Southwest. It consisted of many different tribes and numerous linguistic groups. The Muscogee were probably members of the Mississippi family.

The Muscogee or Maskoki,[3] derived from the Algonquin term for swamp or open marsh land,[4] was an Indian nation living on land bordering the Savannah River, the Atlantic, the Gulf of Mexico, the Choctaws and Chickasaws on the west, and the Cherokees on the north.[5] Whether they crossed the Mississippi is uncertain. Albert Gatschet, who studied languages used by different tribes in an effort to determine Indian tribal relationships,[6] said the Muscogee did not cross the Mississippi.

Three centuries ago the Muscogee were predominately in power over all their neighbors and seemed to have inhabited the south from time immemorial.[7] They had a larger number of tribes than any nation in North America. A tribe was formed when several clans united into one town and lived under one chief. The Muscogee were particularly noted for absorbing other groups, and they increased their number and strength by accepting survivors of conquered tribes and assimilating broken remnants of other nations. Because there were so many streams in their territory, the English called them "Creeks."[8]

There are various stories as to the origin of the Muscogee people. One states that there were two mounds of earth in the forks of the Red River west of the Mississippi where this tribe first found itself. To escape wars, it travelled eastward toward the rising sun and settled below the falls of the Chattahoochee, spread out to the Ocmulgee, Oconee, Savannah and along the seaboard. One tradition ascribes their origin to a cave near the Alabama River and another tale states that they descended from the sky.

A curiously-written manuscript with red and black characters drawn on a skin of a young buffalo was found in Fulham Palace, the home of the Lord Bishop of London, who had been ecclesiastical director of the Georgia colony prior to the American Revolution. It was the Kashita Legend as told by Mico Chekilli, head chief of the Upper and Lower Creeks, in Savannah in 1735, and it related the origin of the greater part of the Muscogee people.[9] The myth is not definite as to the place from which the trek started: "at a certain time, the Earth opened in the West where its mouth is." It relates that the Cussetaw Indians wandered eastward toward the rising sun and cites such names as Ogeechee, Ocmulgee, and Coosa. These enabled Mr. Gatschet and others to trace the Indians' journey. The ancient story attempted to explain the mystery of the red man's existence, the origin of fire, the beginning of medical knowledge, the secrets of plant and animal life and the formation of various Indian alliances.

The wanderers finally saw smoke and knew they had reached the town which they had travelled far to find—"the present place the Pallachacula People dwell in and from whom *Tomochichi* is descended." The Pallachacula People made a Black Drink as a token of friendship for the war-minded Cussitaws, told them they must have White Hearts, and took their tomahawks from them and buried them under their cabins. Thus convinced that they all should be one people, they decided to always live together and be loyal to each other. So the Creek Confederacy was formed, with the Muscogees far outnumbering the combined Uchees, Natches, Hitchitees, Alibamous, Seminoles and Appalachians.[10]

Later the Creek Confederacy was divided. Those living toward the mountains were called Upper Creeks, and Coosa was their chief village. The Indians living toward the seaboard were known as Lower Creeks. Coweta was their Red or War Town, and Apalachicola, until superseded by Kasihta, was their White or Peace Town.

Palachicala or Parachukla was a contraction of

Apalachicola—Great Town. It was derived from the Hitchiti *Apalachocoli* or the Muscogee *Apalachicolo* and signified people of the other side, probably referring to the Apalachicola River.[11] When a general peace was proposed, the deputies from all the towns in the Confederacy assembled there to consider the important matter. Later the town was moved a few miles up the river. Indian villages were often shifted due to the lack of sanitation systems or because the soil became exhausted. However, in this case a calamity had befallen the town. A group of Indian traders had sought protection in the Peace Town from hostile Indians. The Council lodged them in a house and went into session to decide what action should be taken. While they were deliberating, a group of Indians surrounded the house, burned it to the ground and all the traders died. Prior to this time no blood had ever been spilled in this village.[12] Later when the naturalist William Bartram visited Apalachicola, the chief trader took him to visit the old village site, pointing out the remains of the burned house. The American botanist said it must have been a famous capital with many inhabitants, judging by the appearance of its artificial mounds and the size and extent of its fields.

Chiefs and warriors gathered at Coweta, the Red Town, to plan their wars or to put captives and criminals to death.

The Creeks occupied the greater portion of Alabama and Georgia, residing chiefly on the Coosa, Tallapoosa, Flint and Chattahoochee rivers in the earliest times. They claimed all the territory south from Savannah to the St. John's River and all the islands thence to Apalachee Bay, and from this line north to the mountains. They were powerful enough to resist attacks of the northern tribes. Several of their towns existed at the time of De Soto's expedition in 1540.[13]

Ferdinand De Soto, a Spanish explorer, like many of the Conquistadores, was very cruel. He enjoyed hunting Indians, and the natives who angered him were thrown to his savage pack of dogs to be torn apart. He burned his captives alive, cut off their hands and noses, hanging or beheading both white and red men to discipline them. He forced Indian slaves, bound by chains, to carry his baggage. In 1541 he crossed the Ogeechee River, arriving on the banks of the Rio Dulce (Savannah River) opposite the great Indian town of Cutafachique. "Identity of the Indians of Cutafachique has been a puzzle. If Henry Woodward is right in his use of the term, they were the Kasihta Indians and so pure Muscogee," according to a U.S. government report.[14]

While at Cutafachique, about twenty-five miles south of present-day Augusta, De Soto saw four canoes approaching. An Indian woman in the first canoe welcomed the explorer in the name of her sister, the Queen, who rode in the second canoe, sitting on cushions and protected by a canopy. The Queen welcomed the Spaniard saying: "Excellent Lord: Be the coming to these shores most happy. My ability can in no way equal my wishes, nor my services become the merits of so great a prince; nevertheless, good wishes are to be valued more than all the treasures of the earth without them. With sincerest and purest good-will I tender you my person, my lands, my people and make these small gifts."[15] Taking a string of large pearls from around her neck, she presented them to him. He gave her a ring of gold set with a ruby as a token of peace and friendship.

Recognizing how much the white man valued the pearls, the Queen informed him that there were many more buried in the tombs of her people nearby and that he and his men might dig them up. They recovered over 350 pounds of pearls.[16] The Queen became angry at the looting and bad conduct of the soldiers, however, so she refused De Soto's demands for bearers and supplies. The Spaniard took the Queen and her handwomen as hostages, permitting the Ruler to carry a box of valuable pearls which he planned to seize later.

Even the pearls were a burden. One of the men who carried a linen bag of pearls weighing six pounds said to a horseman, "You may have them if you will. I'm tired to carrying them." The offer was refused. "If you will not have them, I will not carry them any longer. They will remain here." He untied the bag, whirled it around his head and scattered the pearls in all directions.[17]

The Queen asked permission to go into the woods on a private matter with her attendants. They disappeared.[18] Not even the bloodhounds could track them. Later it was found that they had returned safely to Cutafachique.[19] De Soto's subsequent route is uncertain, but he probably followed the Savannah River to what is today northwest South Carolina. After obtaining burden carriers and supplies from the kindly Cheraw Indians, he is believed to have pushed on toward the Mississippi, passing near the present site of Rome, Georgia before he crossed what is now Alabama.

The Indians were very fond of the woods and streams and they were protective of the graves of their ancestors. They needed land because theirs was a hunting and agricultural society. James Oglethorpe said of them "they have as much Right to their Woods as an English Gentleman to a Forest or a Chace, and they are more necessary to them since the Veneson is the Flesh and that Chiefly feeds them and the Skins of the Deer is what enables them to pay the English for their Goods.[20]

War was serious business to the Indians. They fought hard but when the battle was ended they went home peaceably, knowing that the defeated tribe would return in time to challenge them. If a member of a family were killed, the remaining kin were honor-bound to avenge the death. An Indian would refuse to fight a member of another tribe if he were related to him even though that group was considered an enemy.

The Creeks became so powerful that they had fifty towns and could send 3500 warriors into battle. They defeated the Cherokees, who were much more numerous; they humbled the Choctaws and changed their loyalty for profit or revenge when dealing with the English in Carolina, the French in Mobile and the Spanish in Florida.[21] The Europeans, who were well aware of the

DE SOTO MEETS THE INDIAN PRINCESS

vital importance of winning the Indians as allies, vied with each other to win their favor.

Tomochichi's name, meaning to "fly up"[22] was spelled in various ways: Tomochichi, Thomochichi, Tomachachi, Tomeychee, Tomochacha, Tomo Chachi, Bocahee, Bocachee, etc. This was because the white men spelled Indian names the way they sounded. The young Tomochichi was related to many important Indian chiefs: Coweta, Kasihta, Cheehaw, Palachocolas, and Oconas. His brother was King of the Etiahitas, and King

Oueekachumpa, the White King, was his cousin. He called himself a Yamacraw Creek and the Creeks regarded Tomochichi as one of themselves. Noted Indian historian John Swanton suggests that Tomochichi's first appearance in history, at Pallachucola, indicates that he was Apalachee. Thaddeus Harris states that Tomochichi's Yamacraws were Yamasees and that Tomochichi's ancestors' tombs must have been Yamasee. His mother was probably Creek and his father Hitchiti, Apalachee, or Yamasee.

The Hitchiti, meaning to "look upstream,[23] lived on the lower Chattahoochee River and claimed occupancy prior to the Muscogee. Their language was spoken in Apalachicola and over a considerable portion of the present states of Georgia and Florida. The Seminoles were said to be half-Creek and half-Hitchiti, and they spoke Hitchiti. This tribe, which believed the Yamasees were related to them, was absorbed into and became part of the Creek Nation, but to a large extent the Seminoles preserved their own language and customs.[24] Tomochichi spoke Hitchiti.

The Apalachee, a Muscogee tribe of Florida, lived in southwest Georgia. When De Soto visited them they were agricultural, industrious, prosperous, good fighters, very brave and adventuresome. They resisted the Spanish until after 1600 when they were finally subdued and forced to accept Christianity. The Spaniards built missions and churches west to the Apalachicola River and up to the junction of the Chattahoochee and Flint rivers. Frequently the Spanish would take their

Apalachee friends seeds of strange plants to see how well they would grow in America. The Apalachees' maize was the finest in the country and they produced the first cotton grown in the South.[25] Many of the tribe ran away rather than submit to the Spanish, and some of them married Creek women. Others settled at Apalachicola and merged with the Creeks.[26] They were the tallest of all the southern Indians. Tomochichi was over six feet in height.

In 1566 Pedro Menéndez de Aviles led an expedition up the coast of present-day Georgia to St. Catherine's Island, where he met the ruler, Guale. The story is told that the Spanish explorer and the Indian chief sat on the beach and ate biscuits and honey.[27] They made a friendship pact permitting the Spaniards to build missions and garrisons "to carry the Cross protected by the sword" to the natives. Thus the land northward from St. Andrews Sound to the Savannah River became known as Guale (pronounced "Wallie") and its Indian inhabitants as Gualeans. The racial connection of these red men who spoke the Muscogee dialect is confused by their imperceptible merging with the Yamasees, but there is satisfactory evidence that the Gualeans were of Muscogee stock.[28]

Yamasee, meaning "gentle,"[29] was called *Yamiscaron* in the earliest writings. This name must have come from the Siouan dialect as there is no "r" in the Muscogee language. They originally lived near the southern boundary of Georgia and were connected with the Hitchiti. One group of the Gualeans or Yamasees lived in the interior and were not subjected to the missions or much affected by European influence.[30] The earliest reference placed them on the Ocmulgee River not far from its junction with the Oconee. They seemed to have ranged northeast of these rivers to or even beyond the Savannah, but always inland from the Atlantic Ocean.[31]

Tomochichi told Mr. Oglethorpe a story which had been handed down to him about a white man with a red beard who had arrived at the mouth of the Savannah. According to several accounts, the Muscogees or Yamasees had lived on the sea coast and the white man had come up the river in a barge to Yamacraw. He met the Yamacraw king, probably Mico Audusta, and expressed deep affection for the Indians "from which he hath had the return of much," as the Indians seemed very fond of him. One of the red men was instructed to take to the visitor's ship a written message directing that gifts be sent for the natives. The messenger did as instructed and was given the articles requested. The Indians were amazed and could not understand how a piece of paper could talk. The Yamacraw king liked the red-bearded stranger so much that he requested to be buried on the spot where the two had talked. Between the Savannah River and the Trustees' Garden, in the city which Oglethorpe laid out, was an artificial hill which was said to be the Chief's burial place. In 1760, long after Tomochichi had told the story, the mound was opened so that a street might be built through it. Indian bones were found within.

James Oglethorpe and others of that time said the

white man to whom the Indians referred must have been Sir Walter Raleigh. The English were anxious to establish their claim to Georgia and so wanted to give credit to an English explorer. In 1586 Rene de Laudonnière, a Frenchman, wrote an account of Jean Ribaut's interview with the Yamacraw and dedicated it to Sir Walter Raleigh. As reported in a London newspaper: "Mr. Oglethorpe has with him Sir Walter Raleigh's written Journal, and by the Latitude of the Place, and the Marks and Traditions of the Indians, it is the very first place where he went ashore and talked with the Indians, and was the first Englishman they ever saw."[32]

However, Sir Walter Raleigh never actually touched these shores. The white man must have been Captain Jean Ribaut, the French Hugenot with the red beard, who talked with the King of the Yamacraws.

Tomochichi, who called himself a Yamacraw Creek, was undoubtedly related in some way to all of these tribes.

2

HUNTER AND WARRIOR

In growing to man's estate among his primitive
people, Tomochichi shared their hardships and trials and
won their respect and admiration. The great chief of the
O'Conas, Oueekachumpa, told Oglethorpe that he was
related to Tomochichi and he stated that the Mico was a
"good man, a warrior of reknown and a mighty
hunter."[1]

As the Mico called himself a Yamacraw Creek and
named his home Yamacraw Village, the word Yamacraw
should be a key to his background. The name Yamacraw
is said to be a distortion of Indian words of similar
sound designating "leaders of the lower empire." One of
the provinces named by Francisco Chicora as existing in
1521 in or near South Carolina was called Yamiscaron.[2]
Yamasee, Yamacraw, Yamiscaron, Iamacraw, Americario, Americano and Amercaraii are all intimately related.

The name Yamacraw is probably derived from the
Florida mission Nombre de Dios de Amacarisse, where

15

some of the Yamasees once lived.[3] These Yamacraws resisted the Spaniards so savagely that Bishop Calderon of
Cuba said after visiting them in 1675 that "their only
concern is to assault villages, Christian or heathen, taking lives and sparing neither age, sex, nor estate." When
Tomochichi suggested to Oglethorpe that the two of
them go hunting, the Englishman said the Indian became so excited that he wondered whether the Mico had
in mind pursuing deer or the Spaniards.

The next record of these Yamasees states that they
had fled from Spanish territory and taken refuge in
Carolina with the English, "some Iamacos, a nation
which lived in the province of Guale became offended at
the governor." It is further explained that they left the
Spanish because the Indians "had a grudge against a certain governor of Florida on account of his having ill
treated their chief by words and deeds because the
latter, owing to the sickness of his superior, had failed
one year to send to the City of St. Augustine a certain
number of men for the cultivation of the lands as they
were obliged to do."[4] The Yamasees renounced their
allegiance to Spain in 1680 when the Governor of St.
Augustine ordered the execution of one of their chiefs.[5]
They were permitted by the Carolina government to
settle near Beaufort. Six years later the Indians returned
to the Florida mission, plundered the church and carried
away prisoners.

Other tribes which sought Spanish protection at St.
Augustine grew to resent the Spanish and, being desirous of profiting from English trade, moved north. By

1684 the Americario or Amecario had settled above the Westoe (Savannah River),[6] where they were initially regarded with suspicion because of fear that they were loyal to the Spanish.

The Yamasee revolted in 1687 against Spanish rule and fled northward across the Savannah River. The Census of 1708 specifies that the Pallachula Indians lived on the Savannah in close association with the Yamasees in a town about twenty miles up the river. The Apalachiccolas were settled at Palachocalcis, or Parachocolos Fort, about fifty miles up the Savannah—a confederate town of the Yamasee. These Indians traded deerskins with the Englishmen in return for supplies. An Indian agent was assigned to them. "You are to proceed to ye Palachocalas and inform them of regard the Government hath for them as directed to other towns of Yamasees,"[7] the government at Charles Town ordered.

The Yamasees had taken the lead among those Indians who sought refuge near the English colony of Carolina. Early documents speak of ten Yamasee towns there. The new settlers were given a strip of land back of Port Royal about eighty miles from Charles Town on the northeast side of the Savannah River. This was known as Indian land long after the natives had left it. The red men extended their hunting expeditions as far south as St. Augustine. The Yamasees joined the Creeks and from 1687 to 1715 occupied a very important position and made many defensive alliances for trade concessions with the English. Governor Archdale of Carolina in 1695 described them as "good friends and useful neighbors of the English."

Early traders introduced the Indians to the European way of life and showed them articles which they immediately desired. The English, French and Spanish competed with each other in trying to win the loyalty of the natives and the control of their trade. Some of the traders married Indian women. Many of the red men, including the Creeks and Yamasees, preferred the English trade because deerskins brought more money in England than in Spain or France. Also, the English woolens and bright-colored calicos could be sold more cheaply to the Indians than other goods which the white traders offered. Guns were exchanged for furs and deer skins. One of the miracles of America was the multitudes of white-tail deer which abounded in the forests and thickets from the Atlantic to the western prairies. Thomas Ashe wrote in 1682, "there is such infinite Herds of deer that the whole country seems but one continued Park."[8] So many deer were slaughtered that by the time of the American Revolution deer trading had almost stopped.

The Indian trade grew to such an extent that several tribes agreed to abide by Carolina's bidding for the privilege of buying guns, blankets and other goods in exchange for deerskins. The trade continued to expand, including more distant tribes, and by 1696 entire towns began moving closer to Carolina so that they might be nearer the source of the goods they coveted. The Carolina government used these new allies in its attack against Spanish Florida. Settlements and trading posts sprang up throughout the territory and hundreds of traders competed for the Indian trade. Tomochichi was a great hunter. He must have been a very active trader. Undoubtedly he was a good friend of the fearless, clever white trader Dr. Henry Woodward, who became the leader in the expansion of English trade.

In 1663 when Captain Robert Sanford, an Englishman, sailed from Barbados to survey the coast of Carolina, north of Guale, looking for a suitable place to found a colony, he took with him Dr. Henry Woodward who wanted to study the Indians. At Port Royal the Mico welcomed the doctor and made a place for him beside him on the throne. Captain Sanford took the Mico's son with him to be educated in England and left Dr. Woodward with the Indians so that he could learn their language and study their methods of raising crops. Dr. Woodward, one of the first English settlers in Carolina, was the first interpreter and one of the first Englishmen to plunge into the western wilderness. He knew five Indian dialects, the Spanish language, and understood the ways of the English and the Spanish.

When the Spaniards learned that an Englishman was living in the country they claimed, the Florida governor sent an expedition to capture him. Dr. Woodward was imprisoned at St. Augustine, but he was rescued by an English privateer and forced to spend several months among pirates on the vessel. When a hurricane destroyed their ship, he and several of his companions were rescued by the English ship "Carolina."

Woodward was among the first settlers when

Charles Town was established in 1670. Soon he began to go into the back country to renew old friendships, and before long he had crossed the Savannah River and was mingling with the Guale Indians. In 1674 he set out from Charles Town with Westoe Indian guides. Although this tribe had the reputation of being very fierce, even man-eaters, they treated the Englishman kindly, giving him food, lodging and deerskins.

In 1682 Dr. Woodward and a party of traders arrived at Coweta on the Chattahoochee River. The Spanish, under the leadership of De Chuba and with a force of 250 Indians, set out to capture the doctor as a warning to the natives that they should not deal with him. When De Chuba arrived at Coweta, Woodward and his allies had disappeared into the forest. The trader sent a note to the Spanish captain stating that his followers were not strong enough to greet the Spaniards but that he hoped to meet him later. De Chuba was so angry that he destroyed a half-finished fort before returning to St. Augustine. The Spanish punished any Indians who traded with the English, continually attacked them and refused to sell them any guns.

In the summer of 1685 Woodward again led a dozen Charles Town traders to the important Creek towns of Coweta and Kasihta. The Westoes made an alliance to protect Charles Town from the Spanish. This was an important contribution to the making of an English America because it secured the gateway of the English speaking nation to the interior of the continent during the early and critical years. The English claimed northwest Guale and forbade the Spanish to even come into the Apalachicola country which the latter had claimed for years.

Charles Town resented Woodward's tie with the Lords Proprietor in England and the money he made from trading. They were angry because they knew the doctor opposed Indian slave trade and had warned the red men that they might be sold as slaves across the sea. The doctor lost his office as an Indian agent and became an outcast. Without the trader's guiding hand, friction increased between Charles Town and the Indians and soon actual war broke out. Woodward, protected by his Indian ally, Creek Emperor Brim, played a giant checker game with the Spanish, retreating as they appeared and returning after they left. He made his last journey in the spring of 1686, followed by 150 Indian burden-bearers loaded with pelts. His outfit was attacked by Spanish Indians who killed several of the party. However, Woodward cemented trader friendship with the Lower Creeks.[9] In a short time hundreds of English traders were ranging the forests from the Savannah to the Tennessee and the Yazoo in the distant Mississippi Valley.

The Yamasee Indians had become very dissatisfied with the traders who plied them with liquor and urged credit upon them. The Indians had no money—only skins and slaves. When the red men could not pay their debts, the white men took their families as slaves. They also traded unfairly by charging excessive prices and using short weights.

Tomochichi was a warrior of reknown;[10] therefore, he must have participated and been involved in the Creek and Yamasee wars of his time.

The Creek Apalachicolas hated the Apalachees who were building churches, accepting Christianity, and encroaching on their territory. In 1686 the Spanish burned the three principal towns of the Creek Confederacy: Coweta, Cusseta, and Colonne. The Creeks moved to the Ocmulgee and nursed their hatred. Convinced by the English that he could defeat the Apalachees by strategy, Mico Brim, Emperor of Coweta, took five hundred men and marched against his enemies. Instead of following the Creek custom of attacking at dawn, the Creeks marked their positions by fires, left folded blankets nearby as if warriors were sleeping in them. When the Spanish and Apalachees attacked at dawn and fired their muskets at the blankets, the Creeks sprang from the bushes behind and won a complete victory, capturing practically the whole enemy force. They made an alliance. They acknowledged not merely their "Hearty Alliance," but also their "Subjection to the Crown of England, pledging fidelity to the High and Mighty Ann, Queen of the English, and to all her Majesties Governours of Carolina." In August 1705 the alliance between Carolina and the Creek Indians was ratified by Upper and Lower Creeks at a council held in Coweta Town.[11]

In 1702 Governor James Moore of Carolina determined to drive the Spanish out of North America. His attack on St. Augustine failed but he demolished three missions, all the settlements in his path, and thirteen missions and settlements near Charles Town. He captured fourteen hundred mission Indians and a large amount of booty. The Spanish withdrew to St. Augustine and many of the Christianized coastal Indians followed.

In 1703–'04 James Moore recruited over one thousand Creek warriors from the Lower Creek towns and again attacked the Apalachees and the Spanish. His forces gained entrance to the fort through a church door and burned churches to the ground, destroyed several Apalachee towns, and took over one thousand prisoners. With the missions destroyed, the Apalachee survivors were carried away and sold into the Carolina slave mart. The Indians had taken as many Apalachee prisoners as had the English and they did not hesitate to trade their captives for ammunition and currency. Several hundred Apalachees moved from their homeland and were forced to settle as an English protectorate on the Savannah River.[12] This was one of the most decisive battles staged in America; it left the Apalachees so weak and feeble that they could not help the Spanish or hurt the English. Moreover, it meant that Oglethorpe's little colony was safe from a Spanish attack from the interior.

The Tuscaroras from across the upper Carolina border in 1711 attacked Low-Country settlements and, "flying like demons from house to house,"[13] massacred one hundred thirty settlers of all ages. John Barnwell and a small band of white men and numerous friendly Indians set out in pursuit of the Tuscaroras. They killed and captured many before returning home. Almost immediately the hostile Indians made a second attack. James Moore, with forty white men and eight hundred Indians, finally located them on the Taw River. After a few hours of siege, he took the fort, killed two hundred and captured eight hundred whom his savage allies sold as slaves.

Emperor Brim, chief of the Creek Confederacy,[14] was a very influential and gifted leader. He resented the coming of the white man because he wanted to keep the land for the Indians. In 1715, angered by grievances against the English traders and encouraged by the French and the Spanish, the Yamasees joined Mico Brim in an attempt to wipe out all foreigners. This was called Brim's War or the Yamasee War. Brim's plan was to destroy Charles Town and then to move against the French in Mobile and the Spanish in Florida. He sent messengers among the northern tribes seeking their cooperation. The Cherokees, influenced by Governor Moore's diplomacy, murdered the secret envoys in their villages and then went out to attack the Creeks.

The plan failed. Charles Town defeated the Indians, but about two hundred settlers were killed and many homes were destroyed. The English burned the Indian sacred spot Ocmulgee Old Fields, in Georgia. At least fifty percent of the Yamasee population was killed. During the conflict the Apalachicolas were seldom distinguished from their Yamasee allies and after their defeat they retired into the Creek Nation instead of seeking Spanish protection as did many of the Yamasees. They settled at the junction of the Flint and Chatta-

Middle Georgia Historical Society, Inc.

EMPEROR BRIM
Sketch by Mrs. Lamar Harrell for General Walter
B. Harris' *Here The Creeks Sat Down.*

hoochee rivers but the greater proportion moved further north.[15] Brim and his followers moved back to their old seats on the Chattahoochee. The Apalachees, Oconees, Uchees and Savannahs moved to the Ocmulgee and then to the Chattahoochee as far as the Tallapoosa to protect themselves against reprisals.[16]

Mico Brim fought no more with the white men, but he used his influence to keep the Creeks powerful. He played the English, French and Spanish against each other and sought by cunning strategy to keep them all weak. He accepted presents from the French, entertainment from the Spanish and favors from the English. Once he said, "As soon as the Present [gift] is wore out, the Talk [of friendship] is forgotten."[17] His people revered him and endeavored to follow his teachings.

By this time Tomochichi was a mature and wise leader. He applied reason rather than passion at the Indian councils. The Yamasees were divided in their loyalties; some favored the Spanish, some, the English. Brim's son Sepeycoffee was loyal to the Spanish; another son, Oulette, had given his allegiance to the English.

After the Yamasee War the tribes under the protection of St. Augustine continually raided English settlements and endeavored to incite the Creeks against them. The Creeks sought an alliance with Spain and gave that country permission to build a fort at Coweta. The Carolina Assembly sent Colonel Theophilius Hastings and Colonel John Musgrove to Coweta with a pack train of presents.[18] When Sepeycoffee arrived with the Spanish to start building a fort, he found his father in conference with twelve Englishmen seeking peace with the Creeks. Brim desired the old-time peace-and-plenty with the English. The Mico gave his niece Coosaponakeesa, his sister's daughter, in marriage to Johnny Musgrove, the half-breed son of Colonel Musgrove, as a royal pledge between Brim and the English. The Spanish, very angry, withdrew.

The Creeks refused to make peace with the Cherokees, remembering the Creek Indians they had killed when Brim sought their assistance in attacking the English. As long as the Cherokee War lasted the Lower Creeks would do nothing to force the Yamasees to make an English peace. The Creek Leader suspected that the English were supplying the Cherokees with guns and inciting them against the Creeks while making friendly overtures toward his people.

On July 8, 1721 the Lower Creeks went to Charles Town and signed the first English treaty "Articles of Friendship and Commerce Agreement" with His Excellency Robert Johnson, Esq., governor and commander-in-chief of the province. Indians signing were: Oboyhathey (Hobohatchey), King of the Abeikas; Youbolomico, the Coosa King; Fannemiche, King of the Oakfuskees; and Tichkonabey—all Upper Creeks. Lower Creeks signing were Tomochichi of the Pallachucolas Town, Tuccaftanogee, mico of the Pallachicolas; King Hott of the Eusitchees; and King Hubble Bubble of the Cheehaws.[19]

The Treaty provided that Englishmen who robbed or murdered Creeks or damaged Creek crops and horses were to be punished by the English; Creeks were to be given ammunition to use against their enemies, providing the enemies were not at peace with the English; Creeks were to protect English goods and traders; English trade rates were to be fixed; Creeks were to apprehend and return runaway slaves; Creeks were to avoid coming to English settlements without permission of the Carolina governor; Creeks were not to encourage any but the English to settle among them; Creeks were to have no further correspondence with the Spaniards. Apparently the English gave verbal assurance that they would not settle south and west of the Savannah River.[20]

The Yamasees killed Oulette, Brim's son, because he evidently had lifted his voice against them in council. Mico Brim was then honor-bound to seek revenge against the Yamasees. The English, being unsuccessful in making peace with the Yamasees, were urging the Creeks into war against that tribe. Colonel Charlesworth Glover sent out Upper Creek war parties under Johnny Musgrove to take Yamasee scalps. Brim continued to maintain his doctrine of neutrality playing one nation against the other. However, he did send out a war party led by Sepeycoffee against the Yamasees to get scalps and thus avenge the death of his son.

The majority of the Upper and Lower Creeks were opposed to a Spanish alliance but were too divided to launch a full-scale attack. Having failed in their anti-English plans, they agreed to make peace with the Cherokees. Carolina sent out an expedition which destroyed Yamasee towns near St. Augustine. Brim was now convinced that the Spanish could not protect the Yamasees so he yielded and the Creeks agreed to break with the Yamasees.

Records state that one *"Tamachi"* accompanied Chekilli to St. Augustine in 1728 when an unsuccessful attempt was made to obtain a Yamasee break with the Spaniards.[21]

Emperor Brim died between 1730 and 1733.[22] Sepeycoffee, who was to follow his father as emperor of the Creeks, died in a fit of drunkenness. Chekilli, the head warrior at Coweta, was chosen to be Brim's successor.

Unfortunately the Yamasees had fallen into disfavor with the Spanish, the English and their Indian allies.

3

TOMOCHICHI AND OGLETHORPE

The failure of the attempt to win a Yamasee break with the Spanish and the consent of the Creeks to break with the Yamasees probably resulted in the banishment of the band of mixed Creeks and Yamasees at Coweta led by Tomochichi, who had opposed the Creek-Yamasee division, presumably in 1728. Other possible reasons were: the Indians became angry at Tomochichi's refusal to join in the Yamasee War; a political disagreement; his enemies may have wanted to be rid of him; or, finally, it may have been a voluntary exile. Tomochichi may have become weary of the constant disputes and decided to seek a place where there would be peace and where he would be close to the land of his ancestors. Before the Yamasee War the Apalachicola tribe had been located upon the Savannah River about fifty miles up-stream. Tomochichi may have belonged to some refugee Yamasee among the Apalachicola and wanted to return. He said: "I was a banished man. I came here poor and helpless to look for good land near the tombs of my ancestors."[1]

There was no suggestion of punishment or mis-conduct. Oueekachumpa later told Oglethorpe that al-though banished from his nation, Tomochichi was a good man and a great warrior. The Indian chief did not talk about his exile. He felt no bitterness toward the Indians and they, likewise, none toward him. The Mico's hereditary status and rights, according to Indian custom, were recognized and he and his immediate followers were allowed to live by themselves. As there was no Spanish deerskin trade, the banished wandered in the woods near the Carolina frontier trading where they could. They "tarried for a season with the Palla-Cholas."[2] Chekilli, who said he was related to Tomo-chichi, claimed that although he had been banished from his nation, he was a good man and had been a great warrior. It was because of Tomochichi's wisdom and courage, he added, that the banished men had chosen him for their king, the Mico of Yamacraw Village.[3]

Charles Town had given permission to Johnny and Mary Musgrove to establish a trading post at Yamacraw in 1732. Their business had flourished.

Nearby Tomochichi set up his Yamacraw Village. It was close to the land of his ancestors, his hunters had

access to a trading post, and as the Mico and the Musgroves must have been closely associated in the past, he
was near friends. In 1732 the Yamacraws asked permission of the government of South Carolina to remain in
their new home. This was granted, as is attested in the
following affidavit:

> Samuel Everleigh of Charleston in the province afore-
> said maketh oath that the tribe of Indians (which
> this deponent hath been credibly informed are
> partly composed of Creeks and Yamasees) settled
> themselves at a bluff called Yamacraw some years
> since and that about the beginning of the year 1732
> some of them came to Charlestown aforesaid and
> desired his excellency Robert Johnson, Esq. then
> governor, that they might have leave to settle there
> and have a trader amongst them; which his excel-
> lency granted and that Tomo-che-chee (who was
> lately in England) was one of them to the best of
> his remembrance and further saith not Samuel
> Everleigh. [Sworn to January 3, 1736.] [4]

The Indian town had a population of forty or fifty
hunters, seventeen or eighteen families, about two
hundred Creek and Yamasee Indians.

Senauki, the Mico's wife, was a clever woman, although not beautiful, and she was devoted to her husband. The Chief's pride and joy was Toonahowi, his
adopted heir, the son of his brother, the King of the
Etichitas. The boy was very intelligent and much
interested in the English and their ways. Tomochichi

wanted his nephew to be taught the English language and to be instructed in the Christian faith.

In 1733 the Creeks divided into several small villages and claimed all the islands upon the sea, and the mainland from the mouth of the Savannah to the Choctaw and Florida Indians. The Spanish sovereignty which had flourished for over one hundred twenty-five years had vanished. The coastal country had been depopulated by wars and the departure of the Spaniards. The islands were known as "Hunting Islands" and were only visited by the Indians at certain seasons for hunting and fishing. The Yamacraw Indians were the only tribe living within fifty miles.

In England at this time an important venture was being planned: the establishment of a new colony between South Carolina and St. Augustine. The main character in its creation was to be James Edward Oglethorpe, but he could not have succeeded without the help of the Indian Tomochichi.

Mr. Ogletorpe was born in London on December 22, 1696.[5] His family was old and prominent in English history, known for its loyalty to the Crown. He was educated at Eton and Oxford and at sixteen accepted an army commission to fight against the Turks. When his father and older brother died, he was left in charge of the large family home, "Westbrook" in Godalming, Surrey. He served in Parliament for many years and was very active in local government affairs. The poverty, unemployment and difficult times in London concerned him, particularly after his friend Robert Castell, a well-known architect,

died after being cruelly mistreated in a London debtors'
prison. This induced him to assist in the preparations for
the founding of the Georgia colony. His mother's death
on June 19, 1732 left him without any domestic ties, so
he agreed to accompany the colonists to their new home.[6]

On January 13, 1733 the passengers on the "Good
Ship Ann" sighted the alien land which was to become
their home. The ship docked at Beaufort on January 20,
where the passengers occupied temporary quarters while
their leader set out in a small boat to locate a suitable
place for the settlement. Governor Johnson of South
Carolina had chosen Colonel William Bull to help Oglethorpe because of his experience in making settlements,
in dealing with the Indians, and because of his thorough
knowledge of the countryside.[7] He resided at "Ashley
Hall" plantation and was the first of his family to be
born in America, where his father had helped plan
Charles Town. The Colonel was well known among the
Indians as an explorer and an outstanding trader.

There is controversy as to whether Colonel Bull
accompanied James Oglethorpe when the spot for the
settlement of the little colony was selected. Mr. Oglethorpe stated in a letter to the Trustees that he had gone
himself to select the place.[8] Another reference states
that Bull did not select the site of Savannah; Oglethorpe
himself selected it, although he may have been advised
by Bull and others.[9] Other sources claim that the two
men together selected the site.[10]

Rounding a bend about fifteen miles up the
Savannah River, the men pulled their boat up on a

narrow beach and climbed the forty-foot bluff which towered above them. Oglethorpe wrote the Trustees on Feb. 10, 1733, telling them about the site he had chosen.

> I went myself to view the Savannah River. I fixed upon a healthy Situation, about Ten Miles from the Sea. The River here forms a Half-moon, along the South side of which the Banks are Forty Feet high, and on the Top a Flat, which they call a Bluff. The plain High ground extends into the Country Five or Six Miles, and along the River-side about a Mile. Ships that draw Twelve Feet Water can ride within Ten Yards of the Bank. Upon the Riverside, in the Center of the Plain, I have laid out the Town, opposite to which is an Island of very rich Pasturage, which I think should be kept for the Trustees Cattle. The River is pretty wide, the Water fresh, and from the Key of the Town you see its whole Course to the Sea with the Island of Tybee, which forms the Mouth of the River, for about Six Miles up into the Country. The Landskip is very agreeable, the Stream being wide, and bordered with Woods on both sides.[11]

Ten days later he added:

> I chose the Situation for the Town upon high Ground. Forty Feet perpendicular above High-water Mark; the Soil dry and sandy, the Water of the River fresh; Springs coming out from the Sides of the Hills. . . . it is sheltered from the Western and Southern Winds (the worst in this Country) by vast Woods of Pine-

trees, many of which are a Hundred, and few under Seventy Feet high. There is no Morse on the Trees, tho' in most parts of Carolina they are covered with it, and it hangs down Two or Three Feet from them. The last and fullest Conviction of the Healthfulness of the Place was, that an Indian Nation, who knew the nature of this Country, chose it for their Situation.[12]

Oglethorpe knew that an ancient treaty between the Creeks and the Governor of Carolina provided that no white settlements were to be made south of the Savannah River without Indian consent.[13] It would be necessary to gain permission of the Mico of the Yamacraws before they would be allowed to establish their settlement. There was a Crown trading post called Musgrove Cowpen a short way up the river belonging to John and Mary Musgrove, both part Indian, whom the Yamacraws trusted and with whom they did their trading. As they had much influence with all the red men and with Charles Town, the couple had been sent word of the coming of the Englishmen and had been instructed to help them.

After walking for some time the group emerged upon a cleared area and noted a big, weathered bark trading house on the river bank. Standing in the doorway, watching their approach, stood a small half-breed Indian woman about thirty-five years old, not more than five feet tall, wearing a red petticoat and an

Osnaberg shift. Her glistening, well-combed black hair,
hanging in two long braids, was tucked into the sash
loosely tied around her waist. A band of beads encircled
her forehead and a feather was stuck at the back of her
head. Her dark brown eyes regarded the newcomers
questioningly as she quietly awaited their approach.

She informed the strangers that her husband was
not at home and asked the purpose of their visit. Oglethorpe replied that the Great King across the ocean had
instructed him to find a place to settle a new colony and
that he sought permission of the Mico of the Yamacraws
for his little band of white people to take up residence
on the Bluff.

The Englishman knew he would need the help of
someone who spoke the Indian language who would be
able to grasp his ideas and make them clear to the
natives. Mary Musgrove appeared to have a quick mind,
and her past association with both red and white men
could be very useful to him. So he offered to pay her
one hundred pounds annually if she would be willing to
interpret for him and help him in his dealings with the
Indians. Mary liked the tall, serious, handsome Englishman and felt that he would be a friend to the red men,
so she agreed to his offer. She lead the strangers to
Yamacraw Village that they might meet with Mico
Tomochichi.

There they were met by a dark mahogany-skinned
Indian over six feet tall, all muscle, who, despite his almost ninety years, walked straight and tall. His body
was naked from the waist up to his collar of rich brown

OGLETHORPE

otter skins. His head was closely shaven except for a plaited scalp lock tucked over his left ear. Several loops of copper were suspended from his right ear. He wore a breech cloth, buckskin boots and leggings. A pouch holding knives, pipes and tobacco hung from his side. Mrs. Musgrove presented Tomochichi to the white man.

Mr. Oglethorpe told the Chief that the Great King across the ocean had instructed him to bring the settlers to find a new home. They wished to be free and able to care for themselves and to be friends with him and his people. He admitted that he knew that the land had been granted to the Indians by the English Crown with the provision that no white men were to settle on the southern side of the Savannah River unless the Indians gave their permission. He asked that he might settle his people close by, promising that they would not interfere with the Yamacraws and adding that they would like to trade blankets, hatchets and guns with the natives.

Tomochichi was not happy to see the white men. He knew that the Indians had suffered cruelly from their association with invaders who coveted their land and their game, and who might even force his people into slavery. Like his kinsman Chief Brim, he wanted to keep the country for the red men. However, he had seen much warfare; he knew there were many, many white men; that they had guns and were stronger than his subjects. Was it possible that if the Indians joined the newcomers they could learn their ways and thus become stronger? The Indians watching the exchange between the leaders showed much uneasiness. Mary Musgrove quieted their fears and finally convinced them of the newcomers' friendly intentions and of the benefits the Indians might receive if they withdrew their opposition.[14]

The Mico finally agreed, explaining that "Creeks and Yamasees followed me when I decided to make our village of Yamacraw. I am their father. By the will of my people, I am also a king." He also said that he wanted his adopted son Toonahowi to learn the ways of the English, to speak their language and to acquire knowledge of their God. So the Chief gave permission for the colonists to settle on the Bluff, but he warned Mr. Oglethorpe that it would also be necessary to gain the consent of neighboring and more powerful tribes. He offered to send runners to them to ask their consent.[15]

"Bring your people to our woods and as soon as they are settled we will call to welcome them," declared the majestic Indian.

The Englishmen thanked the kind Mico as they parted at sundown. The white men hastened back to their boat to return to Beaufort to inform the colonists of the success of the mission. The colonists were instructed to prepare to sail to their new home. James Oglethorpe did not realize then that the two Indians to whom he had talked, Tomochichi and Mary Musgrove, or Princess Coosaponakeesa as she was called, were to prove the best friends the colony at Savannah would ever have. Without their help it probably would not have survived.

As a noted historian later wrote,

Had Tomochichi turned a deaf ear to Oglethorpe and refused his friendship, denied his request, inclined his authority to hostile account, instigated a determined and combined opposition not only of the Yamacraws but also the Uchees and Lower Creeks, the perpetuation of this English settlement would have been either seriously imperiled or abruptly terminated amid smoke and carnage.[16]

4

THE GEORGIA COLONY

Tomochichi must have instructed his scouts to watch for the arrival of the colonists, for as they approached the landing site on the afternoon of February 12, 1733, they were greeted by a volley of small arms, which they returned. Peter Gordon, an upholsterer who was to be bailiff of the new colony, kept a journal in which he recorded the happenings.

About an hour after our landing, the Indians came with their King, Queen, and Mr. Musgrove, the Indian trader and interpreter, to pay their compliments to Mr. Oglethorpe, and to welcome us to Yamacraw. The manner of their approach was thus, at a little distance they saluted us with a volley of small arms, which was returned by our guard and thane [then]

43

the King, Queen, and Chiefs and other Indians advanced and before them walked one of their generals,
with his head adorned with white feathers, with rattles
in their hands to which he danced, observing just time,
singing and throwing his body into a thousand different and antike postures. In this manner they advanced
to pay their obedience to Mr. Oglethorpe, who stood
at a small distance from his tent, to receive them. And
thane conducted them into his tent, seating Tomochachi upon his right hand [and] Mr. Musgrove, the
interpreter, standing between them. They continued
on conference about a quarter of an hour, and thane,
returned to their town, which was about a quarter of
a mile distance from the place where we pitched our
camp, in the same order as they came.[1]

Peter Gordon and a few others had been ill and
were not able to complete the pitching of their tents.
Mr. Musgrove invited them to Yamacraw Village to stay
at his house. As soon as the Indians learned that there
were strangers at the trader's house, they gathered
around a big fire opposite Tomochichi's home and
began to entertain the guests.

"Their manner of dancing is in a circle, round the
fire, following each other close, with many antick ges-
tures, singing and beating time, with their feet and
hands to admiration," related Mr. Gordon.[2]

The next day the colonists were frightened when
they heard much shouting and the beating of drums,
and then saw a large group of Indians appear. The men
seized their guns and all rushed to Mr. Oglethorpe's tent.
"The Indian King & Chi [Chiefs] desired to talk with

Mr. Oglethorp," Mr. Gordon noted in his journal.[3] The medicine man was again in the lead, his face and body painted red, blue, yellow and black. He wore deer horns on his head, a deer skin was thrown over his shoulder and he carried a large fan of eagle feathers with the handles decorated with small jingling bells. As he came forward he jumped into the air, then crouched to the ground, and then straightened up with a high leap into the air. Most of the Indians wore white feathers in their hair as a sign of friendship and peace. Two chiefs marching in front of Tomochichi carried long white tubes decorated with white feathers in their left hands, while in their right hands were cocoanut shells containing shot which they used to beat time as they marched. They would stop several times as they were singing and then

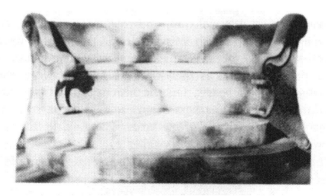

SITE OF OGLETHORPE'S TENT

Memorial bench on present Bull Street in Savannah marks the spot where Georgia's Founder spent his first night ashore. *Gift of the Georgia Society, Colonial Dames of America, in 1906.*

start again as they began a new song. This was their way
of recording tribal history by relating the exploits of
their ancestors.

"May there always be peace between your people
and our people," they chanted as they stopped before
Oglethorpe and waved the white wings over his head. He
conducted them into his tent, seating Tomochichi upon
his right while Mrs. Musgrove stood between them. Mr.
Oglethorpe was presented a lighted pipe of tobacco
from which he smoked several puffs, then passed it to
the Mico and two of his chiefs. Each puffed four times,
blowing smoke to the left, to the right, straight up and
straight down. The Englishman asked the interpreter to
inquire if the King desired to speak first.

Tomochichi said:

"We are glad that you and your people have
arrived safely. We welcome you to Yamacraw. I am no
stranger to the English. My father and grandfather were
well known to them. We have come to welcome you as
we promised. This is the skin of a buffalo. He is the
strongest of all beasts. On the inside you will see the
painted head and feathers of an eagle. It is the swiftest
and fartherest flying of all birds. The English are the
strongest of all people. Nothing can withstand them.
They have a swift and far flight like an eagle. The eagle's
feathers are soft and signify love. The buffalo robe is
warm and promises protection. We hope you will love
and protect our little families."[4]

"We thank you, Great Chief. My people have come

PLAN OF SAVANNAH

Prepared in 1734 for the Trustees "by their Honours Obliged and Most Obedient Servant, Peter Gordon."

a long way and we thank the Great Spirit for bringing us safely here," responded Oglethorpe.

The Mico said that one of his people had been killed by the Uchees but that they would not make war upon them unless the white man was willing. The English leader replied that all wanted to live in peace and he promised the Indians his friendship and that he would try to protect them. Tomochichi then gave Oglethorpe some deerskins which were the Indians' most valued possession. The white man asked that a treaty might be made in which the Indians would grant them the land between the Savannah and Altamaha rivers. The Mico said that there was much land and he was willing, but such a treaty must be agreed upon by the other Creek tribes. He offered to send runners requesting that they meet with the great White Chief. Mr. Oglethorpe gave the Indians presents which pleased them very much and then they returned to their own town in the same manner in which they had come.[5]

Peter Gordon wrote:

> Sunday we hade Divine Service performed in Mr. Oglethorp's tent by Reverd Doctor Herbert with thanksgiving for our safe arrivall. Mr. Musgrove, the Indian trader and his wife were present, and Tomo Chachi, the Indian King, desired to be admitted which Mr. Oglethorp readily consented to and he and his Queen were seated in the tent. During the time of the Divine Service, several of the Indian warriors and others sate at a small distance from the tend, upon trees, and behaved very decently.[6]

The first law passed for the administration of the

Georgia colony, March 21, 1733, was "An Act for Maintaining Peace with the Indians in the Province of Georgia."[7]

May 14–18 Oglethorpe took the Mico and Toonahowi with him to Charles Town. The Englishman was a showman at heart and he realized it might be valuable publicity to introduce his new Indian friends to the English. The interest and eagerness expressed when he presented the red men to the white men impressed him so much he began to consider how valuable it might be to take them to London.

With the assistance of Tomochichi,[8] Oglethorpe invited fifty chiefs and braves, representing eight of the principal Creek tribes, to come to Savannah. This was one of the greatest acts of diplomacy handled by Tomochichi. None of the English officers in Carolina or Georgia had gained Chekilli's consent to a treaty allowing the English to settle on their land. Tomochichi's influence made him Oglethorpe's ally.

Upon returning to Savannah, Oglethorpe found visitors awaiting him. The chiefs of the Coweta, Cusseta, Osweeche, Chehaw, Echeta, Pallachucola, Ocona and Eufaula tribes, as well as the chiefs of the Upper and Lower Creek and the Uchee nations had arrived. Some of them had travelled more than five-hundred miles to enter into a Treaty of Friendship with Mr. Oglethorpe. There were fifty-six chiefs and warriors led by Youhowlakee, the Mico of Coweta and his ward, Essabo, Brim's son and Mary's close kin. All were dressed in full costume, eagle feathers standing high on their foreheads and falling in festoons down their backs. Their faces and the upper parts of their bodies were painted red, blue and yellow. They wore rings in their ears and necklaces of animal teeth around their necks. Their buckskin skirts were decorated with paintings edged with a heavy fringe which came below their knees. They wore buckskin stockings and moccasins.

The colonists fired a volley of gunfire. Some of the Indians had never heard cannons before. Oglethorpe wanted to impress them with the power of the English. Men with guns lined the way on each side of the bluff to the meeting place.

The Indian chiefs were seated on each side of Mr. Oglethorpe. Mary Musgrove, the interpreter, stood in front. About eighty Indians sat on the floor smoking tobacco.

Tomochichi rose and spoke:

"I was a banished man. I came here poor and helpless to look for good land near the tombs of my ancestors, and the Trustees sent people here. I feared that you would drive us away for we were weak and wanted corn, but you confirmed our land to us, gave us food, and instructed our children. We have already thanked you in the strongest words we could find, but words are no return for such favors, for good words may be spoken by the deceitful as well as by the upright heart. The Chiefs of our nation are here to thank you for us and before them I declare your goodness and here I wish to die. We all love your people so well that with them we will live and die. We do not know good from evil, but desire to be instructed and guided by you that we may do well with and be numbered among the children of the Trustees."[9]

Lakee, Mico of Coweta, stood up and said,

"We are come twenty-five days' journey to see you. I have often been advised to go to Charles Town but would not go down because I thought I might die on the way, but when I heard that you had come, and that you were good men, I knew you were sent by Him who lives in Heaven, to teach the Indians wisdom. I, therefore, came down that I might hear good things, for I knew that if I died on the way I should die in doing good and what was said would be carried back to the nation and our children would reap benefit of it.

"I rejoice that I have lived to see this day, and to see our friends that have long been gone from amongst us. Our nation was once strong, and had ten towns; but we are now weak and have but eight towns. You have comforted the banished and have gathered them that we'd scattered like little birds before the eagle. We desire therefore to be reconciled to our brethren who are here amongst you, and to give leave to Tomochichi, Stimoiche, and Illispelle to call the kindred that love them out of each of the Creek towns, that they may come together and make one town. We ask that the Yamasee may be buried in peace amongst their ancestors, and that they may see their graves before they die; and their own nation may be restored again to ten towns."[10]

Chief Oueekachumpa of the O'conas then spoke:

"We agree to share our land with the white men who are the children of the Great Spirit. We thank you for your kindness to Tomochichi who was banished from his people. He is a good man—a great warrier. We have heard that the Cherokees have killed some Englishmen. We will go to the Cherokee country, destroy their harvest and kill their people."

After the three chiefs had concluded their remarks, Emperor Chekilli welcomed the colonists and said that he hoped they would instruct the Indian children in the language and ways of the white men.

These Indians acknowledged their racial affinity with the Yamasee and regarded the Yamasees and Yamacraws as original members of the Creek Confederacy. The English did not dispute the kinship of the Creeks, Yamasees and Gualeans and their right to the lands which they claimed and of which they wished to gain possession.[11]

Oglethorpe thanked the Indians for having come so many miles to the Council and said that he would relay to the Trustees their request to be instructed in the white men's ways. He denied the report about the Cherokees and concluded by thanking them for their affection.

Eight buckskins, one for each of the tribes represented, were delivered to Oglethorpe. In return each chief was presented a lace coat, shirt and hat; and a musket and ammunition were given to each war captain. A barrel of gun powder, four cags of bullets, a piece of Irish linen, a cask of tobacco, pipes, eight cutlashes with gilt handles, tape and ink of all colors and eight cags of rum were to be carried back to their towns; one pound of powder, one pound of bullets and as much provisions for each man as he pleased were allotted the red men for the journey home.[12]

Tomochichi signed the Articles of Friendship and Commerce on May 18, 1733,[13] which permitted Oglethorpe to settle his colonists. The Indians had ceded to the British all rights to the lands between the Savannah and Altamaha, as "far up those rivers as the tide flowed" except for a small place above Yamacraw Bluff where the Indians would make their camp when they visited Savannah, and Yamacraw Village. The islands of Ossabaw, St. Catalina and Sapelo were reserved for bathing and hunting. Also the red men promised not to give any encouragement to other white men who might want to settle among them.

They also agreed to accept fixed prices upon articles of trade consented to by both parties; that anyone murdering, robbing, wounding or injuring the Indians would be tried and punished according to English law, upon proof of same; if the Treaty were not kept, trade should be withdrawn from the offending town; the land not used by the Indians might be used by the white men, but all lands as agreed upon should be reserved for the Indians; any Indian doing harm to the white men would be tried upon proof, by the English law; Indians should be rewarded for returning run-away slaves; the Indians, as they had promised, were to give no encouragement to any other white people but the English to settle among them and they were not to have any correspondence with the Spanish or French. A schedule of prices of goods was agreed upon: i.e., one gun for ten buckskins, one hoe for two buckskins, etc.[14]

Satisfied, most of the hunter-warriors disappeared into the forest. The rest remained for a week, supplied during that time with provisions from the Trustees' store.

Oglethorpe sent the Articles of Friendship and Commerce to the Trustees for their approval. He wrote that "If the French be allow'd to destroy our Indians, Nation by Nation in time of Peace, the Settlements must follow in the first of a Warr."[15]

He taught the Indians how to throw back the French hand grenades and how to keep themselves in the open fields or behind trees. After a two-day conference with the Creeks he commented, "I am a red man, an Indian, in my heart; that is why I love them."[16]

The White Leader knew that when the Indians mentioned revenge they meant war, and he could not let that occur. In June 1733 an Indian shot himself. Some of his friends found him and claimed the English had shot him and declared they wanted revenge. Tomochichi tried to pacify them. "Shoot me," he said, baring his chest. "If you desire to kill anyone, kill me, I am an Englishman."

Later they found that the dead Indian had been in a dejected mood. An Indian boy admitted that he had seen the warrior pull the trigger with his toe and shoot himself.[17]

The White Chief ordered one of the Carolina boatmen who was drunk and had beaten an Indian to be tied to a gun until he was sober and then he was to be whipped. Tomochichi asked Oglethorpe to pardon him, but the latter refused to do so unless the beaten Indian requested it.

"O Foneka," said the Mico, "this Englishman being drunk has beaten you. If he is whipped for so doing, the Englishman will expect that if an Indian should insult him when drunk the Indian should be whipped. When you are drunk, you are quarrelsome and you don't like being whipped."

Foneka asked Oglethorpe to release the man. His request was granted. Tomochichi and Foneka untied the man, probably to show that he owed his safety to their intercession.

Tomochichi was very compassionate. He learned that many of the colonists were sick and lacked fresh provisions. He went hunting with ten Indians, shot game and sent it to those who were sick. When he later learned that his gifts had not been received, he went hunting again and this time distributed the game himself to the poor and sick. "The first gift had not been put to proper use so I distributed it myself the second time," he replied when asked about it.[18]

"You need fear nothing. Speak freely," the English leader told the Indian.

"I always speak freely; what should I fear? I am now among friends, and I never feared among my enemies," was the reply.[19]

To make certain the Indians were not only friendly but stayed friendly, Oglethorpe actively engaged them on Georgia's side. He arranged to hire a number of

Tomochichi's men to hunt and fish for the colony. Two companies of forty men each were organized with compensation of one bushel of corn a month, one blanket a year as payment in war or hunting and a gun per man upon enlistment.

The Indians would pitch their tents only a hundred paces from the town. When the colonists heard singing and the drums, they knew a hunting party had just returned safely, and that the fish or game would be shared with them. The settlers liked to go fishing or oystering with the Indians, who used torches or made bright fires in their canoes to attract the fish. Some of the fish, especially the mullet, would be drawn to the light and would jump into the boat. At low tide Tomochichi and the Yamacraw Indians would make a fire on one of the small islands in a salt creek where oysters abounded to roast the oysters while the tide was low. Later they collected the roasted oysters and feasted upon them. The Indians furnished guides for exploration parties and taught the older boys to stalk deer and bear. Tomochichi encouraged good feeling between the two races and on every occasion exerted his influence in behalf of peace and justice.

Both the spiritual and the temporal foundations of the Colony were firmly established on July 7, 1733[20] when the colonists observed Savannah's first Thanksgiving Day. Tomochichi, Mary Musgrove and some trappers from Augusta were guests. All the inhabitants assembled on the strand at daybreak; prayers were read; the settlers then proceeded to the Square where a house and lot were assigned to each freeholder. A plentiful dinner of fresh beef, turkey, venison, vegetables and English beer followed. Later a business meeting was held during which court officers were appointed, a jury was impanelled and a case was tried. Then came talk, merry-making and dancing. By nightfall the Indians returned to their camp and the trappers left. Georgia's first Thanksgiving Day had ended.

Among the many diverse immigrants who settled in Georgia were the Salzburgers, a group of Protestants whose religious beliefs had caused them to be driven from Austria.[21]

"You may stay with us here in Savannah or settle your own town," offered Mr. Oglethorpe.

"You will have more people coming all the time," replied their leader, Baron Von Reck. "Since we want to farm and be independent, another settlement might serve us. But let us be nearby."

"Good! I will have Tomochichi show you the best land available and if you don't mind, I'll come along," said Mr. Oglethorpe.

The Mico gave the Salburgers two hunters to supply the newcomers with food; his highest war chief, Tuskenovi, to keep them company; and then he and Oglethorpe helped them lay out their new town. The newcomers had chosen a site on a crooked, sluggish little creek about 25 miles up the river from Savannah. Both the town and stream were named *Ebenezer*, which means "the stone of help."

"I visited the Indians and their King, Tomochichi.

I gave them some raisins which they liked very much,"
Baron Von Reck wrote in his diary.

Although Oglethorpe made his own decisions and
was a strict disciplinarian, the settlers respected him and
called him "Father." The natives liked and esteemed
him, partly due to their Mico's love and affection for
him but also because they knew he was a fair man. They
referred to him the settlement of such things as a controversy between the Uchees and the Lower Creeks.
Feelings were so aroused that a general war threatened
between the two tribes. They asked the White Leader to
decide the matter. His decision was accepted and peace
was restored.[22]

An important part of the Indians' education was
the enduring of hardships, so they admired and respected the manner in which Oglethorpe met privation.
He lived in a tent on the strand a little west of Bull
Street during his first year. Then he moved into the
cottage built by Joshua Overind, a forty-year-old
mercer, who had come on the "Ann" but had died four
months later. The house had one room, a single bed, a
table, and a couple of rush-bottom chairs. This was his
home during the remainder of his stay in Savannah.
Oglethorpe ate mouldy bread, drank boiled river water,
and in general set an example as one who could endure
hardships.

Tomochichi was the firm friend of the white man,
the guide, adviser, protector of the colonists, and the
constant companion and faithful friend of Oglethorpe.
He had proved himself by his liberal grants of territory;

by furnishing the colonists with venison, wild turkey and other items; by procuring interviews with the chiefs of the Upper and Lower Creeks, winning their allegiance to the English, and being willing to help the white men in their difficulties with the French and Spanish.

5

TOMOCHICHI IN ENGLAND

James Oglethorpe, beset by many problems, decided early in 1734 that it would be wise for him to return to England. The Trustees resented the heavy financial drain on the treasury, the scarcity of reports from the colony, and some were even beginning to lose interest in Georgia. The settlers were complaining. He remembered how interested the Charles Town people had been in the visit of Tomochichi and his nephew. Furthermore the Chief had expressed a wish to visit England. "I want my beloved Toonahowi to be taught the way of the English and to ask the Good Fathers to send teachers for him and our Indian children. To see the home of you, my good friend, the King, and the Proprietors is my fondest dream," the Mico had confided to Oglethorpe.

Would this not be a golden opportunity to grant the Mico's desire and also to rekindle interest and enthusiasm for the struggling little community on the Savannah River! How opportune it was that the Trustees had invited Tomochichi to proceed to England for the formal ratification of the Articles of Friendship and Commerce.

The Creeks had prepared for the fomal ratification of the Treaty by sending a bundle of eagle feathers from town to town so that all the villages might register the Pact. These were given to Tomochichi to be delivered to the King. The selection of the Indian guests was not easy, but finally Tomochichi announced his choices. He would be accompanied by his wife, Senauki; Toonahowi, his nephew and adopted son; Hillispilli, the war chief of the Lower Creeks; Umphechi, Senauki's brother, a Uchee Chief from Palachocolas; and five chiefs of the Cherokees, their attendants and an interpreter.[1]

The party left Savannah on March 23, 1734.[2] While in Charles Town awaiting a ship for London, the Indians entertained the townspeople with a lively ball game and in the evening they participated in a war dance before the Governor's palace.

The group sailed from Charles Town on the "H.M.S. Aldborough,"[3] on April 7 and reached England on June 16. The Trustees sent a sleek, many-oared barge manned by liveried boatmen down the Thames to pick them up and bring them to London.[4] A hasty trip was made to Oglethorpe's estate at Godalming. On June 27

James Oglethorpe wrote Sir John Philipps from St. Helen's near the Isle of Wight:

> There appears as though a door has opened for the conversion of the Indians; because a superior or chief of the Indians, Tomo-cha-chi, the Mecko of Yammacraw, a man with an excellent mind, is so desirous of having his young people instructed in the science and wisdom of the English, and consequently in the Christian religion, that he came over with me in spite of his advanced age in order to find ways and means for instructing his people. He is staying with me now, and he has brought with him a young boy whom he calls his nephew and immediate heir. This child has already learned the Lord's Prayer in the Indian and English languages. I shall leave the Indians on my estate in the country until I go to the city, where I shall have the pleasure of calling on you and of reporting on further happenings which may please and amaze you.[5]

When the party arrived in London the city provided a festive welcome. Bells rang in honor of the colorful visitors; there was a tremendous bonfire; and many demonstrations of welcome. Their every move was reported by the newspapers.[6] They received gifts, invitations and even salutations in poetry.

In the last category were these lines:

What stranger this? and from what region far?
    This wonderous form, majestic to behold?
Unclothed, yet armed offensive for the war,
    In hoary age, and wise experience old?

His limbs inured to hardiness and toil
    His strong large limbs, what mighty sinews brace!
Whilst truth sincere and artless virtue smile
    In the expressive features of his face.
His bold, free aspect speaks the inward mind,
    Awed by no slavish fear, by no vile passion blind.[7]

A beautiful set of apartments at the Georgia Office had been furnished for the visitors.[8] The Trustees decided the expenses were a national charge in the interest of the government to protect the colony from the Spanish and French. £1000 was authorized, allowing £600 for the Indians' maintenance and the remainder to be spent for presents. The expenses of Tomochichi's visit totalled £1079 5s.[9]

The Indian delegation was formally presented to the whole body of the Trustees on July 3. Senauki, the only woman in the group, attended the reception. The Earl of Egmont noted in his diary that she was an "old ugly creature" who dressed the Indians' meat. In a contemporary painting of the scene by Dutch artist William Verelst, however, Senauki has a kind face and an alert expression. She is depicted in a long scarlet English dress with her hair done up in English fashion and wearing a small rose tucked behind one ear. Her gracefully crossed

The Henry Francis duPont Winterthur Museum

TOMOCHICHI MEETS THE TRUSTEES
Senauki *(in long dress, at right)*, and Toonahowi *(center)* are immortalized with the Mico *(right of center)*, some of their Yamassee friends, and the Trustees in this historic painting by William Verelst.

hands and the dignity of her bearing indicate that even in such unfamiliar garb in a foreign land she was completely at ease. That she and her painted, half-naked male companions were accurately portrayed is indicated by Egmont's notation that the figures "were very like."

The Earl went on to give a detailed description of the historic meeting between the Trustees and the Indians:

Tomochichi advanced to the lower end of the table,
the rest of the Indians standing round, with the Interpreter explaining. He began by excusing himself if he
did not speak well and to right purpose for when he
was young he neglected the advice of the wise Men,
and therefore was ignorant. That he now was old and
could not live long, wherefore he desired to See his
nation Settled before he died. That the English were
good men, and he desired to live with them as good
neighbours, for which reason he came over to talk
with us, but he would not have done it were it not for
Mr. Oglethorps Sake, whom he could trust, and who
had used him and his people Kindly. That he thank'd
the Great Spirit (at which word he pointed & looked
upward) that had brought him Safe hither, and he
hoped would carry him Safe back.

I answered him in the Same manner paragraph
by paragraph that the interpreter might explain. That
we all had the Same God & fear'd him, that we lived
under a good and gracious King, who does justice to
all his Subjects, and will do the Same by his friends &
Allyes, as we would do on our parts. That we will
look upon his children to be ours, and ours theirs, and
Should be ready to hear any proposition they would
make when they thought proper. After this, We all
rose, and took each of them by the hand, which I
Saw delighted them, & then call'd for wine and
tobacho to entertain them.[10]

The Mico then gave the Trustees as a token of
friendship twenty-five buckskins, "one Tyger Skin and

Six Boufler Skins."[11] The Earl of Egmont gave Tomochichi a silver snuff box which the Indian said he would
wear around his neck on a string close to his heart. He
also was given a large elaborately-carved gilt tobacco
box. Oglethorpe gave the Trustees a fine black horse
about seven years old. A canoe was presented to the
Queen.

"He is a handsome and bright boy," the Earl said
of Toonahowi to the great pleasure of his adopted
father.

The Archbishop of Canterbury received them at
Lambeth Palace with tenderness and kindness.[12] Toonahowi recited the Lord's prayer in English, and the
churchman inquired of his guests about their religion.
The Indians, being superstitious, refused to answer; they
believed that some calamity would befall them if they
expressed their views on the subject. Later they attribu-
ted the death of one of their companions to their having
spoken too freely since their arrival.[13] The Archbishop
was so polite that he would not sit down during the
audience, although he was so weak that he had to be
supported by two of his clergymen. The Mico noted this
and excused himself from making a speech he had
prepared. "I will speak to Dr. Lynck, your Grace's son-
in-law," he said. The prelate thanked them for coming
and expressed the hope that something could be done to
teach the Indians Christianity. Later Tomochichi had a
conference with Dr. Lynck and declared his joy in believing some good persons would be sent among them to

instruct the youth. In all respects the red men were very pleased with their reception.

The next day they dined at "Charlton," the Earl of Egmont's home. The president of the Georgia Trustees wrote in his Journal:

> On the 19th they all dined with me at Charlton. I entertained them with dancing, & Musik, made them presents and walk'd them in the wood, which much delighted them as it put them in mind of their own country. At table I ask'd Tomochachi what dish I Should Serve him? He reply'd that he [would] eat whatever was Set before him, meaning a civility thereby that he would not refuse anything I should offer him. They also had the respect not [to] eat when Served until my wife and I had taken the first mouthfull. They had learn'd the way of drinking and bowing to the company, and behaved with much decency, making no noise or interrupting anyone that Spoke, and the Same is observed by them when they sit in Council. . . . At parting he [Tomochichi] told me that he came down to See me with a good will and return'd in friendship. That God above would continue it, and he hoped we would take care to make their children Christians.[14]

King George II and Queen Caroline received them at Kensington Palace on August 1st. The Indians wished to wear their own clothing but Oglethorpe insisted on re-outfitting them. The Mico and his Queen wore long scarlet robes trimmed with gold braid and fur, two of

Savannah Public Library

KING GEORGE II   **EARL OF EGMONT**

These notables were among the dignitaries who received Tomochichi and his friends on their memorable visit to England.

the party wore blue, and three were dressed in yellow—all trimmed with fur. Their faces were painted—some black, some half-red, and some with triangles and bearded arrows on their chins instead of whiskers. They wore moccasins, and feathers in their hair. Three royal coaches, drawn by six horses each, took them to the palace. There Sir Clement Cotterel, master of ceremonies, presented them to the King and Queen on their thrones.

Johnny Musgrove, the half-breed one-time swamp warrior who now was a prosperous trader among the Yamacraws, translated the speeches, speaking in an ele-

vated tone and in the strange accents of the Indian
orator.

Tomochichi addressed the King:

> This day I see the Majestry of your Face, the Great-
> ness of Your House and the Number of Your People.
> I am come for the good of the whole Nation call'd
> the Creeks, to renew the Peace which was long ago
> had with the English. I am come over in my old Days,
> and I cannot live to see any Advantage to myself, I
> am come for the Good of the Children of all the Na-
> tions of the Upper and of the Lower Creeks, that
> they may be instructed in the Knowledge of the
> English. These are the feathers of the eagle, which is
> the swiftest of birds and who flieth all round our
> nations. These feathers are a sign of peace in our land.
> They have been carried from town to town there; and
> we have brought them over, to leave with you, O
> great king, as a sign of everlasting Peace.[15]

His Majesty answered:

> I am glad of the Opportunity of offering you [an ex-
> pression] of my Regard for the People from whom
> you come, and am extremely well pleased with the as-
> surances you have brought me from them, and accept
> very gratefully this Present, as an Indication of their
> good Disposition to me and my People. I shall always
> be glad of any Occasion to shew you a mark of my
> particular Friendship and Esteem.

Tomochichi then turned and spoke to Her Majesty:

> I am glad to see this Day, and to have the Opportun-
> ity of seeing the Mother of this Great People. As our
> People are joined with your Majesty's we do humbly
> hope to find you the common Mother and Pro-
> tectress of us and all our Children.[16]

The Queen replied graciously.

Senauki also made a speech.

Toonahowi said the Lord's Prayer in English for the King and Queen, and she stroked his face and invited him to come to see her again for she had a present for him. He replied to her in English.

Later the Chief was asked what he had seen at Court. He replied that his hosts had taken him through many houses (rooms) to make him believe the King's Palace consisted of several establishments. When he noted with surprise, however, that he returned by the same stairs he had already used, the Mico realized that it was all one house. He said that although the English knew many things his people did not know, he doubted that they were happier.[17]

The Indians were shown the sights of London: the Tower of London, Greenwich, Hampton Court, the Royal Garden, hospitals and public buildings. Excited throngs gathered along the way to observe them. When visiting the Boys' School at Eton, the visitors received every mark of respect from the Rev. Mr. George, Dr. Berriman and the rest of the Fellows. On closing their visit to the school room, Tomochichi asked that the lads might have a holiday when the doctor thought proper, which caused a general huzza. They were shown several apartments of the college and took a respectful leave.[18]

The red men were especially fascinated watching the Changing of the Guard, paying particular attention to the King on horseback while he viewed them. The barges on the Thames on Mayor's Day intrigued them.

When the Indians were ill, Mr. Oglethorpe sent his personal friend, the great physician Sir Hans Sloan, to take care of them. Umphechi, Senauki's brother, died of small pox. The White Chief took the red men to his estate where they could grieve together away from curious eyes and bewail their dead as was their custom. The Earl of Egmont noted in his Journal:

> This month one of the Indians died of the Small pox. Sr. Hans Sloan attended to him. He was cosen to Tomachachi. They Sat up all night bewayling his loss. On this occasion Tomachachi told Mr. Verelts that his Relation was gone to the Great Spirit and he would See us no more, but he Should See him, and believed he Should be the first.[19]

The Uchee Chief was entombed in the churchyard of St. Johns, Westminster.[20] It is thought to have been the first burial of an American Indian chief on British soil. His body was sewn up in a blanket and bound between two boards according to Indian custom. His clothes, glass beads and some pieces of silver were buried with the body. Tomochichi, some of his domestics, the parish church warden and the grave digger were all who were present when the body was lowered into the grave. "We are not weeping because this one has died, but because he has not lived to see the day we are waiting for on which greater knowledge will appear to us," replied Tomochichi when asked why the Indians mourned so much.

The Indians were entertained at many of the great houses of London. The Archbishop of Canterbury sent an elaborate barge down the Thames to pick them up and take them to dine with Lady Dutry, a benefactress of the Georgia Colony. They were entertained in a handsome manner. On leaving the Chief said to his hostess through his interpreter, "O Gracious Lady, could I but speak English, I would tell you the thoughts in my heart. I am touched by this noble reception you have given me and my people, but I am more pleased to be able to thank you for your help in sending white people to Georgia."

The Trustees appointed a committee to confer with Tomochichi to determine what he would like done for his people. He requested that rules and regulations be set up for weights and measures in trading Indian goods, deerskins, and other pelts. In justification of this application he stated that he had paid ten pounds of leather for a blanket at Yamacraw.[21] He asked that traders be licensed; that store houses be established in every principal village where the natives could be supplied at a fair price for such articles as they wished to purchase; that if the Indians were cheated they might have means of restitution; that rum not be sold to the red men; that his nephew Toonahowi and other children be given teachers to instruct them in religion and the English language; and that they be given the picture the "Great Lyon they Saw at the Tower"[22] to be placed in a great hall they intended to build. It was promised that these requests would be given careful and immediate attention.

The Indians went to see Prince William, the Duke of Cumberland, perform on his trained horse, after which the famed horse guard passed in review before them. Prince William gave Toonahowi a gold watch, admonishing him "to call upon Jesus Christ every morning when he looked at it."[23]

The Mico kept in touch with his people while he was in England. The Trustees wrote Causton that

> Tomo Chachi desires that Icko (Jehko?) Saona or Savannah, and Mahokly the Uchy Indians may stay till he comes back, and that You would let them know he is doing a great deal of Good for them and their Children; and you are to let them have what Corn they want as usual.[24]

William Verelst painted a portrait of a grave and commanding Tomochichi with his left hand resting upon the shoulder of his adopted son, who held an eagle in his arms (*see* Frontispiece). The Mico had taken to England this symbol of his own royalty. The picture was hung in the Georgia Trustees' room. One Herr Kleinschmidt of Augsburg, Germany, later made an engraving of the painting, a copy of which was given to The Georgia Historical Society by George W. Wylly.[25]

The Trustees signed the "Articles of Friendship and Commerce Agreement" on October 7. James Oglethorpe uttered a sigh of relief. Fewer than twenty years had passed since the bloody Yamasee War in which the Creeks had joined to attack the white settlers of Carolina. His colonists, isolated and outnumbered, could meet a similar fate at any time. Keeping peace with their Indian neighbors was a matter of life and death. The direct result of the treaty was the pacification of all the Lower Creek Indians, the Uchees, and the Yamacraws— all tribes which acknowledged English supremacy. Later the pact was recognized by the Upper Creeks and the Cherokees. For years the stipulations were preserved inviolate and the Colony of Georgia was permitted to extend its settlement up the Savannah River and along its coast.[26]

Londoners, much impressed with the dignity, conduct, and intelligence of the Indians, no longer considered them savages. Tomochichi was called wise, liberal in his views, a man of integrity, a philosopher, a statesman, a brave-hearted warrior, and one of Georgia's noblest sons. Philip Thicknesse had a profound regard for the Mico, saying "His ethical qualities were far superior to those of many Christians."[27] Another commentator wrote, "although Tomochichi was never in Ireland, he must have kissed the Blarney Stone."[28]

Mr. Oglethorpe was also honored. The Queen questioned him about the colonial silk production; the King studied maps and charts with him; the press and people praised him saying that his pains and efforts in founding Savannah would make him famous in history. A chapel was named in his honor and his likeness was engraved on a medal. He refused an appointment as governor of South Carolina because of his friendship with the incumbent, Robert Johnson. However, he did accept a commission for administering the "Act for Maintaining Peace with the Indians."[29]

The White Leader emphasized the constant threat of Spain and France. £25,800 was given him to build a chain of twenty forts. The Trustees also favored the laws which Oglethorpe supported: prohibiting the sale of rum, outlawing slavery, and maintaining peace with all Indians in Georgia.

Tomochichi said his dream of visiting England had been fulfilled beyond his wildest hopes. Having been in London for four months, he petitioned the Board saying "That tho' all Travellers in their country are entertained without any Expense, I am sensible while we stay in England they must be a charge to the Trustees, and as the Cold Weather is coming, I am desirous of returning home."[30]

The Indians sailed for Georgia on October 31, 1734,[31] on board the "Prince of Wales" laden with many gifts and mementoes valued at more than £400.[32] The Chief said to Oglethorpe as he left,

> I am glad to be going home, but to part with you is like the day of death. You have never made a differ-

ence between our people and your people. You have
never broken a promise to us. When I die I want to be
buried in the white man's town and not in the
forest.[33]

The Indians arrived in Savannah in December, as
Tomochichi wrote the Trustees:

We arrived Safe at Savannah on the 28th of Decem-
ber last. We have all had our health during the whole
Voyage Except Toonanahoure whom we fear'd would
have Dyed & thro he is now much better yet is Very
Walk and Infirm we have Rec'd All olr Goods & were
Very Kindly used by the Capt.[34]

The Indians gathered to greet them and to hear
about the wonderful things they had seen, the strength
of the English nation, the generosity of their hosts, and
the royal welcome accorded them. Tomochichi distributed the gifts and mementoes. Oglethorpe had instructed
Mr. Patrick McKay, the Indian agent in Georgia, to support Tomochichi in all things. The Agent regularly
handed over to the Mico for distribution to his people
assorted presents which had been sent from England.
Tomochichi was very generous in giving away all of the
rich presents and retaining none for himself, being more
pleased in giving to others than in keeping any. All of
these things helped to firmly establish Indian good will
toward England and the Colony.

The Trustees awarded John Musgrove £100 in cash

and five hundred acres of land as reward for his services as interpreter. This, together with his trading business, made him Georgia's most prosperous citizen.

A letter of thanks "which I writt from Tomochichi's words" was sent by Noble Jones to the Trustees.

> I thank the Hon. Trustees for the many favours they have bestow'd upon me. We have been kindly Used by the Capt. which we shall endeavour to Return by our love as well to ye Captain as to all the white people who Now are or Shall hereafter be known to Us. We have lately delivered some skins which we desire your Honours to Accept as a token of Gratitude & love. We are Sensible that your Honours have Much better things, but as they are few in Number hope the Skins will be Acceptable.[35]

The Trustees ordered that the skins be dressed and sold for the uses of the Trust.[36]

A year passed before Oglethorpe, taking care of Colony business, was to leave London. The English people were so impressed and enthused by the visit of the Indians that the return trip of the White Chief was called the Great Embarkation Many persons wanted to join the colonists, and two hundred and fifty-seven actually made the trip.

6

THE INDIAN PRINCESS

Mary Musgrove, the attractive young half-breed who had agreed to act as interpreter for Oglethorpe proved to be a loyal and invaluable friend to the Colony. She was born a Creek princess about 1700, at the Coweta Town on the Ocmulgee River, which was then the chief town of the Creek nation.[1] Her Indian name was Coosaponekeesa, and she was a niece of Emperor Brim, the famous chief who had plotted the Yamasee War.

When the Princess was ten years old, her English-trader father took her to live at Ponpon, South Carolina,[2] among the English people. In 1715 the Yamasee War broke out and Chekilli advanced as far as the Stono River. Perhaps the Princess decided that she would prefer a life of freedom among the Indians to the restric-

tions of living among the civilized English, so she joined
her uncle the War Chief and his retreating forces.

In 1716 the government of South Carolina sent
Colonel Theophilius Hastings and Colonel John Musgrove
on a mission to Coweta with a train of presents[3] to attempt to gain the friendship of the Indians and thereby
the neutrality of the Creeks. John Musgrove, Jr., a tall
and attractive young man who was part Indian, who had
served on various missions among the red men, accompanied his father. When Brim had dallied in breaking
with the Yamasees, Colonel Glover had sent "Johnny,"
as he was often called, to take Yamasee scalps. His
father won an agreement that the Indians were not to
hold any rights to the land or to kill any cattle between
Charles Town and the Savannah River. As a regal seal to
the new peace with the English, Chief Brim gave his
niece Princess Coosaponekeesa in marriage to John
Musgrove, Jr.

At the time of her marriage the bride spoke four
languages—English, Creek, Yamasee and Cherokee. She
took the name Mary Musgrove, and for seven years she
and Johnny remained in Coweta Town. In 1723, following the birth of the first of Mary's four sons—not one of
whom lived to maturity—the couple moved to Carolina.

Nearly ten years later, having received permission
from Governor Johnson to build a trading post on
Yamacraw land on the south side of the Savannah River,
they moved to the site given them. Their post, called
"The Cowpen" because of the cattle they raised there,
consisted of a big trading house, "A good house, 2

Viewpoint Publs., Inc.

MARY MUSGROVE

hutts, nearly fifty acres of clear'd land, part of it Pine land, part Oak and hickory."[4] Living in seclusion, they built up their trade and established credit with Charles Town. The Musgrove trading post was an imporant contact in negotiations with the Indians. Mary claimed they received 12,000 deerskins annually, one-sixth of the amount taken in at Charles Town. Soon they were wealthy.

James Oglethorpe held Mary in high esteem because of her influence with the Indians. She was a woman of prestige, means and vivid imagination. She was also generous in giving the colonists meat, bread, liquor and every necessity which the Musgrove plantation offered or which could be purchased on credit from

Charles Town. One historian later called her the "Poca-
hontas of Georgia."[5] The Musgroves' trade would have
increased had they not worked so steadily to keep the
Creeks faithful in their alliance with His Majesty's subjects. Almost daily their hunters were employed in some
expedition in behalf of the settlers, and many of them
left to help in the Spanish skirmishes and were killed.
Mary helped Oglethorpe establish cordial relations with
Tomochichi and other Indian chiefs. She quieted their
fears and helped the Yamacraw Mico gain their consent
to friendly agreements with the colonists.

Full responsibility for the Cowpen and its activities fell upon Mary when John Musgrove served as interpreter for Tomochichi and his friends on their visit to
England. During that period she experienced difficulties
with her husband's partner, Joseph Watson.[6] He quar-
reled frequently with her, and finally Mary took him to
court for calling her a witch and for trying to shoot her.

Subsequently Watson was tried and found guilty of
beating an Indian. This was a very serious offense because the colonists could not afford to incur the ill will
of the Indians. Watson was already unpopular with the
red men because they felt he tried to cheat them. One
day some natives came to the Cowpen to have their
skins weighed. Watson locked the door and refused to
let them in. Mrs. Musgrove persuaded the man to leave
for fear the Indians would kill him when they did get in.
When the Indians found that their quarry had escaped,
they were so angry that Esteechee, one of the Indians,
killed the Musgrove Indian slave named Justice.[7] The

colonists took Esteechee to the town limits and told him not to return as they were afraid the red men might come to his aid. Watson was also urged to leave but he refused, saying the colonists were trying to steal his share of the Musgrove store.

"If I do not get my fair share, Tomochichi and his Indians will be held as hostages by the Trustees," Watson warned.

Arbitrators were appointed to determine Watson's holdings in the store.

A brave named Skee, whom Oglethorpe had appointed captain of the Indian militia, became Watson's drinking companion. Causton, Savannah bailiff and storekeeper, accused the trader of keeping the Indian drunk because he was afraid of him. Watson boasted that Skee would die when he became sick with fever, and when this unhappy event transpired the red men accused Watson of killing him. The Indians thought that Esteechee planned to murder Watson in retaliation if the English law did not interfere because it was a very serious offense for an Indian to kill a white man. A clever solution resolved the dilemma: Watson was judged to be a "lunatik" to be confined until well and then to stand trial; Mary was compensated for the death of her Indian slave by the gift of a Trustee servant; and presents were sent to the Indians in an effort to reconcile them.

Upon returning from England Tomochichi invited the headmen of the Upper and Lower towns to gather for a big ceremony on June 11, 1735 in Johnson Square to receive presents and to negotiate a definite boundary settlement. Twenty grenadiers and two ensigns marched in advance of the Indians to the roll of drums. Chekilli, emperor of the Upper and Lower Creeks, led the Indian delegation composed of Eliche; King Ousta, head-chief of the Cussitaws; Tomechaw war king; Wali, war captain of the Palachucolas; Peopiche; King Tomehuichi, Dog-king of the Euchitaws; Mittakawye, head war chief of the Okonees; Tuwechiche, king; Whoyaune, head war chief of the Chehaws and of the Hokmulge Nation; Stimelacowechi, king of the Jawocolos (Sawokli); Ewenauki, king; Tahmokmy, war captain of the Eu-fantees; and thirty other warriors. The main body of colonists followed, but as they approached the Square about half of them fell out of line and took a short cut which enabled them to arrive ahead of the procession. Upon reaching the Square the Indians passed through a double line of colonists and were greeted by a salute of seventeen cannons. Awaiting them were Thomas Causton, Henry Parker Bayliss, Thomas Christie, John Vatt, and other men and free holders of the Town.[8]

Tomochichi distributed the gifts which had been sent by the King and Trustees as proof of their benevolence and concern for the red men.

Chekilli then recited the Kasihta Legend. In conclusion he said:

> . . . That they [the Creek Confederacy] Still find the White path for their good for Altho' Tomo-chachi has been a Stranger and not lived in their Town amongst them Yet they See that in his Old age

he has done himselfe and them good because he went with Esquire Oglethorpe to see Great King and hear his great Talk and has brot it to them And they have heard it and Believe it for wch reason they look upon him as the father and Senauki the Mother of them all and are resolved that when he shall be Dead to Look upon Toanhon (?) his Nephew as Chief of them all in his Stead and Hope he will be a great Man and Do good for himselfe And them that their Eyes had been Shut but now were more Open And they believe the coming of the English to this place is for good to them and their children and [the English] will always have Strait Hearts towds them And hope tho' they were Naked and helpless they Shod have more good things done for them.

I am of the Eldest Town and Chosen to Rule after the Death of the Emperour Bream I have a Strong Mouth and will Declare this Resolution to the Rest of the Nations and make them Comply therewith we are glad the Squire Carry'd Some of our people to the great King and his Nation That I am never tyred of hearing what Tomochachi Tells me abot it That all my people return thee great Thanks to all the Trustees for So great a favour And will always do our utmost Endeavour to Serve them and all the great Kings people whenever there shall be Occasion I am glad I have been Down and Seen things as they are We shall go home and tell the Children and all the Nation that the Great Talk wch Tomochachi has had with the Great King and bear in remembrance the place where they now have mett and call it Georgia. I am Sensible there is one who has made us

all And tho' Some have more knowledge and others
the Great and Strong must become Dirt alike.[9]

Cheikilli's speech, curiously written in red and
black characters on a buffalo skin, was translated into
English as soon as delivered. Later it was taken to England, set in a frame and hung in the Georgia office in
Westminster. Subsequently it disappeared, but the
German book *Ausfuehrliche Nachricht von den Salz-
burgischen Emigraten* (Urlsperger, Halle, MDCCXXXV
v. 1 pp. 869–876) has a comparatively accurate version
of the original.

In the conference which followed the welcoming
ceremony the Georgia officials and the Indians, with
Mary Musgrove as interpreter, defined the Georgia limits
as including all the territory south and west of the
Savannah River up to two hours' walk above tidewater
and as far south as the St. John's River. The sea islands
of Ossabaw, St. Catherines and Sapelo were retained by
the Indians for hunting and fishing.[10] It is likely that
there was discussion also of the possible granting of an
additional area for a fort at the falls of the Savannah
River, the site of which is now encompassed in the city
of Augusta.

Mrs. Musgrove was a popular hostess whose fre-
quent visitors included Tomochichi, James Oglethorpe,
Sophy Hopkey, John Wesley and other prominent persons. They were entertained with feasts of wild turkey,
venison, and barbecues. Despite her large household and
the many demands on her time, she willingly taught the

Creek language to such apt pupils as John Wesley, George Whitefield, Bejamin Ingham and Court Chaplain Ziegenhagen.

The former Indian princess faced unexpected trouble when John Musgrove died on June 12, 1735. The Earl of Egmont noted that five hundred acres granted him as an interpreter would be given as promised. "His Son will enjoy it. In the meantime Mary his widow enjoys it, and it has good Improvements on it. The place is call'd Grantham."[11] Evidently two sons had died earlier because the husband and father devised the Cowpen "unto my two Sons, James and Edward Musgrove." Within the next seventeen months these too were taken from Mary. "In the evening of Nov. 23rd I buried Mrs. Musgrove's only son," wrote John Wesley in his Journal. Thus bereft of all her family, Mary was the wealthiest woman in Georgia. She had a flourishing fur trade, a five-hundred-acre plantation, a large number of cattle, and ten indentured servants to care for stock and crops.

In 1735 the Spanish, a constant threat to the colonists, attacked another Georgia party of Yamacraw Indians.[12] Under the necessity of keeping peace, Oglethorpe could not sanction Creek or Yamacraw retaliation. He gained permission from the Crown to establish a line of forts to protect the English settlements, and persuaded Mary to build on the Altamaha River a trading post which she called "Mount Venture."

That Oglethorpe was keenly aware of Mrs. Musgrove's value to the Georgia undertaking is indicated in

a letter dated Durham, England, November 13, 1745, in
which he wrote in part:

> I find there is the utmost endeavor by the Span-
> ish faction to destroy her, because she is of conse-
> quence and in the King's interest; therefore it is the
> business of the king's friends to support her, besides
> which I shall be desirous to serve her out of friend-
> ship she has always shown me as well as the colony.[13]

An historian later wrote,

> If a "talk" was to be held with the Indians at
> Frederica, Savannah, or any other point, nothing
> could be done without the important aid of Mary. If
> warriors were required for the defense of the colony,
> it was through Mary's influence that they were ob-
> tained. Did disaffection, leaning on French intrigue or
> Spanish guile, hold aloft the "bloody stick" and
> threaten the massacre of the inhabitants, her power
> became conspicuous in the soothing of asperated
> feelings, and in the recall of half-alienated affection.[14]

Oglethorpe would not hold a conference or council with the Indians without having Mary present as an
interpreter. He would send for her as far as one hundred
miles and sometimes she would be on these missions for
several months at a time.

The colonial leader assigned twenty Rangers to
protect "Mount Venture." Their commander was Jacob

Mathews, a husky young man of twenty-five who had come to Georgia as an indentured servant several years before. Mary was assigned the responsibility of keeping the Indians friendly while watching for Spanish activity at this post established in the midst of Indian country. Two years after her husband's death, Mary Musgrove was married to the proud and ambitious Mr. Mathews.

Jacob Mathews raised cattle at the Cowpen, cultivated thirty acres of corn and peas for the Colony, built a large house, improved the plantation, entertained as many as fifty Indians at a time, went with Oglethorpe on military forays into Spanish territory, and was a Ranger for four years. Despite these accomplishments, Mary's new husband was to cause her much grief. The Trustees had allotted John Musgrove five hundred acres which were now demanded by Jacob Mathews. Mary had money and property including a house in Savannah, the Cowpen at Yamacraw, "Mount Venture" on the Altamaha and £100 a year which she was to receive as an interpreter. Her husband thereby became a man of means, but he drank continually and became involved in many brawls. He interrupted court, he beat up a constable, he encouraged discontent against authority, and both colonists and magistrates feared him. He influenced Mary to demand more presents for the Indians and more land and money for her services.

A group of Indian traders were living at the Townsend House in Savannah when Mathews and a halfbreed Indian came in and started to quarrel. One of the traders sent for a guard. Mathews insisted that the

Indian be jailed and personally took him to the guard house for the night. The next day Mathews told Oglethorpe that the inn keeper was responsible for the trouble. Townsend angrily said that he had ten witnesses who would support his innocence. Because the White Leader needed the friendship of the Indians and Mary's help as an interpreter, the inn keeper was told to apologize to Mathews or he would lose his license.

The Colony was growing and extending its limits. In 1737 Tomochichi decided to leave Yamacraw Village and build a New Yamacraw a few miles above the old town which would be large enough to accommodate the Savannah and Shawnee Indians who had joined him.[15] On December 13, 1737, William Stephens, Georgia secretary to the Trustees, wrote: "Went to the Old Town and saw a cloth had been spread. Mary Mathews was sitting at one end with two girls, her husband and Tomochichi, nearby. A young shote, barbecued, was set on the table." Mr. Stephens was invited to join the group and he took some wine. This celebration was a treat to Tomochichi and three or four other Indians because the Mico was giving his land, judged to be two hundred or three hundred acres, to Mary and her husband. With Mary interpreting, Tomochichi told Secretary Stephens that he desired notice to be taken of his claim in the land which he was granting to Mrs. Mathews and her husband. He added that he hoped the Trustees would not be offended, but henceforth only Mathews cattle were to be allowed there.[16]

Oglethorpe was in England when Tomochichi announced that he was giving away lands which had been expressly recognized as his by the treaties of 1733 and 1735. Upon returning to Georgia and being asked to approve the transfer of ownership, he replied that the Trustees would have to give their consent. The Trustees, in order to protect their own rights, replied that the Indians would have to cede it to them, and they in turn would grant it to the Mathews. Though the proper action was taken in Georgia, the Trustees delayed so long that Mary and her husband employed lawyers in England to press their claim.

When Jacob Mathews became ill, Mary took him to Savannah for medical attention. While there they received word that "Mount Venture" had been destroyed in a joint attack by Indians and Spaniards. Jacob Mathews died on May 8, 1742. Mary's overseer at the Cowpen was soon drafted for a St. Augustine expedition, thus leaving her place untended. Her cattle were driven off and her establishment and everything there went to ruin. Both her overseer and her brother, Edward Griffin, were killed at St. Augustine.[17]

James Oglethorpe was anxious to do all he could for Mary. When he made his final departure for England in July 1743 he gave her a diamond ring off his finger and £200 as part payment for her services as an interpreter. Their friendship was a sincere one. As long as the White Leader remained with the Colony, the Indian woman continued to be a devoted friend to the settlers and to him.

Oglethorpe had made her feel even more important

than she actually was. Those who followed him in control did not treat her as kindly or with as much tact. She complained bitterly four years after he left, "I have been abused, insulted, and despised by these ungrateful Englishmen who are indebted to me for every blessing they enjoy."[18]

7

JOHN WESLEY

Savannah needed a minister of the Gospel. The Rev. Dr. Herbert had left the Colony three months after the settlers landed and had died on the return trip to England. The Rev. Samuel Quincy, who had next been appointed, submitted his resignation because he could not prevail upon his wife to join him.[1] Dr. John Burton, a Trustee, suggested that John Wesley, a Fellow of Lincoln College of Oxford, a fine classical scholar, and an earnest student of divinity, be appointed to the position.

Mr. Oglethorpe respected and admired the young student's father, the Rev. Samuel Wesley, who had encouraged the settlement of the new colony, and he knew his family to be a fine one.

John Wesley had heard much of the leader of the

little colony at Savannah and he gladly accepted the invitation to meet with him. "I was struck by the pompous appearance of the man, big almost to hugeness, with a wig flowing down his shoulders, heavy jowls, brusque manner—a military man. His voice would mellow in sympathy and understanding," was the way the minister described him.

The young man's large, bright, dark-blue eyes regarded Mr. Oglethorpe thoughtfully. He was only five feet tall, slender, beautifully proportioned; his long, glossy dark hair curled at the ends and hung to his shoulders. He wore a long black coat, knee breeches, and held a three-cornered hat in his hand. At thirty-three he was an ordained priest of the Church of England who longed to be able to work with the Indians.

The young clergyman discussed the matter with his mother, Susannah Wesley, a brave and devout woman. She said, "Had I twenty sons, I should be glad to have them so engaged, though I should never see them more." So he agreed to go with his friend the Rev. Benjamin Ingham as a missionary, accompanied by his twenty-nine-year-old brother Charles, who had been appointed Secretary of Indian Affairs.[2] He was to act as minister in Savannah until the Trustees granted him access to the Indians. The Trustees asked the Society for the Propagation of the Gospel in Foreign Parts to grant Mr. Quincy's £50 per annum to John Wesley whom they would appoint as minister. The Society agreed.[3]

Tomochichi's visit to London had inspired so much enthusiasm and interest in the Savannah colony that two hundred fifty-seven passengers sailed on the "Simmonds" on October 18, 1735. Among those on board were James Oglethorpe, John and Charles Wesley,

THE REV. JOHN WESLEY

Benjamin Ingham, and twenty-five Moravians. The Wesley brothers were one day to be world-famous: John as the founder of the Methodist Church and Charles, the sweet singer of Methodism, as the composer of six thousand hymns.

John Wesley became very fond of the Moravians, spending much time with them. He was particularly impressed by their courage. During a severe storm they showed no fear of shipwreck, convincing him that they had greater faith in God than he did. In his Journal he wrote that Oglethorpe was very good to the passengers, that he seldom ate more than once a day, and then consumed salt provisions so that the fresh might be given to those who were sick. He gave his cabin to Mrs. Welch, an expectant mother, who was ill. It was thought she would die, but she survived. "We can't be sufficiently thankful to God for Mr. Oglethorpe's presence with us," the minister stated. There were many letters from colonists praising their leader for his humanity at sea, and later on land.

John Wesley landed on Cockspur Island on Sunday, February 15, 1736. The young minister prayed for the first time in the New World, giving thanks for a safe journey. This historic spot is marked by a monument topped with a cross.

Tomochichi had asked that Toonahowi and his people be instructed in Christianity. He was very pleased when he heard that John Wesley had been sent to them and sent a message of greeting along with a side of venison, saying that the Indians would be visiting him shortly. When the clergymen were informed that the Indians had arrived, the Wesley brothers put on their surplices, John picked up his Greek testament and then went forward to greet their visitors. He later described the gathering in his Journal.

Josiah Hopkey and his niece, Miss Sophy, welcomed the missionaries. Magistrate Hopkey stepped aside a moment to bring forward a coppery man.

"This is Tomochichi. He is a mighty chief among his people."

John shook the big brown hand. He was very much impressed with the size, gravity, and dignified mien of the Indian.

"I am deeply pleasured," responded the Mico in his favorite English phrase. Although the red man always used an interpreter, there were many who were suspicious as to how much English he really understood.

Tomochichi, Toonahowi, Senauki, two women and three children had come on board to visit them. The Queen proudly wore the scarlet rose dress she had worn at the Trustees' reception in which she had posed for her picture. It had been given her by the Trustees, one of the many gifts given the Indians, and was her most cherished possession. The women were dressed in calico petticotats and loose woolen mantles, their braided hair hanging over their shoulders. Toonahowi wore English clothes. The Chief's face was stained red in many places, his hair was dressed with beads, a scarlet feather was placed behind his ear, a blanket was wrapped around him, the straight folds of which fell to his knees. His erect form and fine grave visage had something of the aspect of an ancient Roman.

The gathering stepped forward to shake hands. John was embarrassed because he knew that the Indians did not permit any man, except her husband, to touch or speak to a woman, unless she were ill. He directed an alarmed glance toward the Chief. The Mico quickly spoke to Mary Musgrove, who then said to the missionary, "It is permissable to shake the Queen's hand, for you are come as friends."[4] The missionary recovered his composure, stepped forward and took Senauki's boney fingers in his.

The Queen had brought a large jar of milk and

another of honey. She said, "I hoped when we Spoke to them, we would feed them with milk for they were but children, and be Sweet as honey toward them."[5]

All of them sat in a semi-circle on the cabin floor except Tomochichi, who began to speak earnestly with great gentleness of voice and manner, gesturing with his hands and head.

> I am glad to see you here. When I was in England I desired that Some might Speak the Great Word to me, and my Nation then desired to hear it; but Since that time We have all been put into Confusion. The French built a Fort with 100 Men in one place, and a Fort with 100 Men in another place, and the Spaniards are preparing for War. The English Traders too, put us into confusion, and have Set our people against hearing the great word for they speak with a double tongue. Some Say one thing of it, and Some another. This does not commend the Christian religion to my Tribe. But we would not be made Christians after the Spanish way to make Christians. We would be taught first, and then baptized. But I am glad you are come. I will go up and Speak to the wise men of our Nation, and I hope they will hear.[6]

When Tomochichi stopped speaking, John Wesley sprang to his feet. The size of the big Indian towering above him did not bother him. He replied, with Mary interpreting,

> Though we are come so far, we do not know whether
> He will please to teach you by us or no. If He teaches
> you, you will learn wisdom, but we can do nothing.[7]

The next day another party of Indians visited the Wesleys on shipboard. The ministers were much impressed with the size, strong bodies, and gentleness of these natives who spoke so softly. The Moravians sought a personal acquaintance with the Mico. They formed a friendship which did not waver as long as both were in the colony.

The captain of the "Simmonds" was afraid to continue to Frederica without a pilot. Mr. Oglethorpe ordered thirty single men of the colony to proceed southward with the sloop "Midnight," taking cannon, arms and ammunition. Tomochichi's Indians were directed to accompany and help the convoy. Because they knew Oglethorpe was in a hurry, the men rowed night and day despite the rough weather, vying with each other to please their leader. He endeavored to relieve their fatigue by serving them refreshments. Realizing how tired the men were, the Indians asked to take the oars. They did very well and introduced a new form—rowing a short and then a long stroke alternately—which became known as the "Yamasee Stroke."[8] Charles Wesley proceeded with the group to Frederica where he had been assigned to be Mr. Oglethorpe's secretary and minister to the St. Simons Island settlers.

John Wesley made his first visit to the Indians shortly after he landed. The missionary called on Mary Musgrove at the Cowpen and then continued on to Yamacraw to visit the Chief, but he was not at home.

The colonists wanted a church, but they had neither the necessary materials nor the money. Oglethorpe held a service before his tent the first morning the settlers were in their new home. Thereafter they worshpped in a tent or in the shade of trees. Later they used temporary structures or public buildings. When John Wesley arrived the worship services were being conducted in the Court House. The people were strongly Protestant, permitting freedom of worship but expecting everyone to attend divine services and to recognize the existence of God.[9] Before many weeks had passed, Tomochichi and his wife were regular attendants, as Oglethorpe wrote the Trustees:

> The Indian King comes constantly to Church, is desirous of being instructed in the Christian religion and has given me his newphew, a boy who is his next heir, to educate.

Mr. Oglethorpe was mainly concerned with the welfare of his fellowmen. He seldom discussed his views on religion, although he had a reverent attitude toward the clergy and repeatedly expressed devout trust in and deep gratitude to the Almighty. John Wesley often reproved him for not being more regular in his attendance at prayer meeting and for not saying more about his religious beliefs, which criticisms were always taken so well that Wesley firmly maintained that Oglethorpe was right.

The Reverend Mr. Wesley often held service on Sunday in four different languages—English, French, German and Italian, and he was studying Spanish so that he could preach to the Jews from Spain. Although Mrs. Musgrove interpreted for him, he wished to learn the Creek language. In 1736 he wrote his first book of hymns and organized a Sunday school in Christ Church Parish. When a child came to Sunday School barefoot

Savannah Public Library

THE REV. CHARLES WESLEY PREACHING AT ST. SIMONS
Probably painted by an English artist who imagined that mountains were a part of coastal Georgia's topographical landscape.

and the children laughed at him, Wesley came to church barefoot the next Sunday. He took the first census, which recorded 518 persons in the colony. Often he was a guest of the Musgroves.

Anything which might jeopardize the friendly relations with the Indians concerned the Trustees. Might a marriage do so? Rumor had it that John Wesley had been sent to Georgia because the Trustees had dismissed the Reverend Samuel Quincy after he had married Joseph Fitzwalter, who was in charge of the Trustees' Garden, and Molly, Captain Tuscanee's oldest daughter and Skee's niece. Tomochichi had given the bride away. The colonists who attended the ceremony said it was a very pretty affair. Mr. Oglethorpe instructed John Wesley to investigate the matter, and the minister later reported that although the bride had not been baptized, most Savannahians were pleased with the intermarriage. The Indians asked that Fitzwalter go into the Creek Nation and trade with them, but the Trustees refused permission.

"To convert the heathen aborigines" had been John Wesley's dream. He was continually setting out on his own, walking, riding horseback, or travelling in a flat-bottomed barge, which was hard going on rough waters. Once he fell asleep on the boat deck and awoke underwater, having rolled off the vessel. Often he rowed a small boat through swamps to reach his parishioners, and many nights he slept on islands miles from any settler. He preached frequently under trees, most memorably under "The Wesley Oak" which still stands on St. Simons Island. Tirelessly he went from village to village, preaching to the people and trying to teach the Indians. They never understood him, and he never understood them. He seemed to get closest to them when he put aside his preaching and just talked to them about life after death.

Baron Von Reck said the Indians had no religious ceremonies and no priests. They believed in a superior being who had created them, Solalycate, "He who sitteth above." They worshipped him and thanked him for having made them. At every opportunity Wesley questioned the Indians about their beliefs.[10] He asked the Chickasaws if they believed God had made the sun and other beloved things.

"We cannot tell. Who has seen?" replied Pausloobee, their spokesman.

"Does God love you?" he was asked.

"I do not know. I cannot see him. We have been too busy fighting to learn from books."

Tomochichi told Wesley that

We would not be made Christians as the Spanish made Christians. They were baptized even when they lied, stole, and murdered. Since my attention was first called to this subject I have closely observed and reflected upon the conduct of those who call themselves Christians. I am not happy with what I find. Yet I am willing to do all I can to help you continue your work and will try to influence and by example to counsel others to listen to your teachings. I have

my doubts where your mission will be successful. But
you have my best wishes.

"There is but one—He that sitteth in Heaven, who
is able to teach men wisdom," said Wesley.[11]

In a later conversation Wesley urged Tomochichi to
listen to the Christian preaching and become a convert.
The Indian retorted scornfully, "Why these are Christians at Savannah. These are Christians at Frederica.
Christians drunk! Christians beat men! Christians tell
lies. Me no Christian!"[12]

Tomochichi commented that the Great Spirit had
given the Englishmen such great wisdom, power and
riches that they wanted nothing. Although the Indians
were given much land, they wanted everything. He
urged the Creeks to resign themselves to the English, to
allow them to settle among them so that they might obtain much-needed supplies. The English were generous,
they would trade with and protect them from their
enemies. He also told the missionary that his father had
been burned by the Spaniards because he would not become a Christian.[13]

The Mico told John Wesley that the conflicting
stories of the French, Spanish and English had confused
the Indians on the subject of Christianity.[14] Wesley,
with Mary as interpreter, tried for an opening with
Chekilli, leader of the Lower Creeks. Chekilli admitted
that the white men knew more than the red men, but he
pointed out the vanity of the English who built big
houses as if they were to live forever. The Chief also

conceded that the Indians lived in sin and did not believe that God would "teach us while our hearts are not white and our men do what we know is not good and, therefore, he that is above does not send us the good book."[15]

John and Tomochichi were dining with Oglethorpe. The missionary asked the Mico what he thought he was made for. The old man replied, "He that is above knows what He made us for. We know nothing." When questioned as to his feelings about prayer, Tomochichi answered that the Indians never prayed to God but left it with him to do what he thought was best for them. Asking for any particular blessing looked to him like directing God; and if so, that must be a very wicked thing. For his part, he thought everything that happened in the world was as it should be; that God of Himself would do for everyone what was consistent with the good of the whole; and that man's duty to Him was to be content with whatever happened in general, and thankful for the good that happened in particular.[16]

John had profound respect for the Mico, even though he felt discouraged because the Indian did not like him. The Chief felt very close to Mr. Oglethorpe and always had much to say when in his company, but he said little when Wesley was present. The missionary would have felt more kindly toward the Indians if he had been free to go among them. Whenever Wesley spoke of going to the Indians, Oglethorpe objected. He feared the young minister might be intercepted or killed. When he had difficulty restraining him, Mr. Oglethorpe said, "You cannot leave Savannah without a minister!"[17] Wesley, who felt that the appointment was made without his solicitation, never got around to accepting his superior's view that his duty was to be a minister and not a missionary.[18] He noted that, "As yet I have neither found nor heard of any Indians on the continent of America who have the least desire of being instructed. The Indians have only two rules—to do what they will and what they can." He thought of them as liars, gluttons, drunkards, thieves, and as opinionated in their own wisdom as the "ancient Romans or the modern Chinese."[19]

Although Mr. Oglethorpe resented Wesley's resistance to public authority, speaking against proceedings of the magistrates in such a manner as to incite rebellion among the people, he felt sorry for him and tried to help him. "Your flock here are babes in the wood, in the Kingdom of God as well as in this wilderness of Georgia. Deal kindly with them," he urged.

The devout Wesley kept himself to a rigid schedule of praying, studying and preaching. His feelings toward Savannah are etched in gold on his monument in Reynolds Square in that city: "My heart's desire for this place is not that it be famous or rich, but that it may be a religious colony and then I can be sure it cannot faile of the blessing of God." However, the colonists rebelled at rising for 5 A.M. services and listening to long sermons which often seemed directed against people in the

Savannah News-Press Photo by Robert Kempf

WESLEY MARKER
Ceremony marking dedication of marker in Reynolds Square, 30 December 1976, which commemorates the Rev. John Wesley's Anglican parish in Savannah. A statue of the founder of Methodism is shown at right.

community. Rules of conduct were strict and communion was denied to anyone who had not been baptized. When Herr Bolzius, the Salzburger pastor, was forbidden to partake of Holy Communion in open church, he stormed out and announced that he would never return.

John Wesley wanted to establish an orphanage in Savannah. He urged his good friend George Whitefield, an eloquent preacher, to join him in Georgia to start such a project. Whitefield sailed for Georgia in 1737 but passed Wesley somewhere on the high seas on his return to England. However, George Whitefield selected the site for the children's home, named it "Bethesda" (House of Mercy) and worked hard for nineteen years raising money in England and throughout the northern colonies to support it.

During Bethesda's first winter, the Spanish pirates seized an English ship which was bringing provisions for the orphans. Tomochichi received word that the boys were crying from hunger. He shared his tribe's precious venison and rice with the starving children.[20]

Meanwhile John Wesley had been attracted to young and pretty Sophy Hopkey, who devoutly attended church and deeply admired the handsome young rector. He gave her French lessons, became her spiritual advisor, and constantly sought her company. He even reviewed the matter of marrying her with his friends the Moravians, who advised against it. Although Sophy gave him plenty of opportunity, he could not bring himself to the point of proposing. The girl became discouraged and accepted the attentions of William Williamson, whom she married. Wesley subsequently denied her Holy Communion because she had become lax in her church duties, an action which so angered her husband that he brought suit against the minister. The people, who were unhappy with Wesley's strict rules, sided with the court. The Reverend Mr. Wesley refused the court

summons when a warrant was issued for his arrest, saying
he was a minister and the court had no jurisdiction over
him. He then consulted Mr. Oglethorpe, who advised,

> I wouldn't take shelter in the cloth. It would show
> you a more courageous man if you faced the court
> and presented your case. But no matter what is the
> solution of the issue, you must realize that your work
> here is finished.

"Very well," John said, "I will meet the court."

After being repeatedly postponed, the case was
finally dropped by mutual consent.

In October 1737, Wesley, believing there was "no
possibility as yet" of instructing the Indians, decided
that God called him to return to England.[21]

During the winter of 1737, one year and nine
months after he had arrived in the Colony, John Wesley
set out secretly in the darkness to make his way to
Charles Town.[22] He was accompanied by Constable
Coates, a man named Gough, and a barber by the name
of Campbell. A servant boy rowed them to Purysburg,
where they landed at three or four o'clock in the morning;
from there they made their way to Port Royal on
foot. The missionary, suffering hunger and thirst,
plodded wearily through miles and miles of marshy,
barren ground. Finally he reached Charles Town tired,
sick and disappointed and boarded the "Samuel." He
arrived in England on Christmas Eve.

8

THE INDIAN SCHOOL

Tomochichi's dream that his people would be educated was about to be realized.

When the colonists came to Georgia his village of Yamacraw was within the present area of Savannah, situated on the bank of the Savannah River between what is now West Broad Street and Musgrove Creek Canal. This land was reserved for the Indians in the treaty made with the colonists and Trustees. Noble Jones, the colony's surveyor, described the land as "bounded by a blazed line (Distinguished by a Red Cross) on ye Eastermost Side thereof Abutting to the Town of Savannah, by a Road or High Way Leading from ye Said Common to ye Plantation of Mrs. Musgrove (Commonly Called Musgroves Cowpen) on the South, by a Creek Commonly call'd ye Indian Creek on ye West, and on the North by the River Savannah."[1]

Tomochichi, recognizing that the gradual increase in the numbers of his people and of the colonists would make it desirable for the Indians to have more space, wrote the Trustees that: "The Savannah Indians are now with me. They have chosen Idsquo to be their King. Idsquo with all his people are Agreed to Joyn me in building on Pipemaker's blough and we intend to live to Gether."[2]

New Yamacraw was about four miles west of Savannah and one mile east of Pipemaker's Creek. It could be seen from Savannah by standing on the bluff, looking up the east side of the river. Like most Indian villages, it was built in a straggling manner. The Public Building was thirty feet long and twenty feet deep. Four houses were put together to form a square with a court in the center. Business was conducted in these houses and each Indian had a place assigned to him "according to his dignity."

Tomochichi's house, built of clay like the others, had three rooms; one room was kept locked, and to it only his closest friends were permitted entry to see his two treasures—a picture of his dear friend James Oglethorpe and the picture of the lion which the Trustees had sent him. In the second room the Mico held his councils; in the third room he entertained his guests with roast pork, buffalo, fowl, pancakes and tea.

It was probably also in the third room that Senauki graciously served tea to Oglethorpe's friend, Mr. Tanner, from Surrey. Mr. Phillip Thicknesse, who was in Savannah in 1736-37, frequently went to New Yamacraw and in the course of these visits he learned some Creek language. He said "I soon became convinced that my person and property were as safe at the Court of Yamacraw as at any court in Christendom nor could I perceive that King Tomo, Senauki, his Queen, and Tonohoi, his nephew and heir were not as happy as any prince of the most polished courts in Europe." Another colonist stated that he had been given a very good

Georgia Historical Society

SITE OF SCHOOL AT IRENE
Twentieth Century archeologists uncover the foundations of Georgia's first school.

dinner of roast and boiled pork at Tomochichi's house
and that Senauki had made tea for him. She probably
had made the dinner also.[3]

Oglethorpe felt that building a schoolhouse near
New Yamacraw Village would help not only the youth
but that it would also afford an opportunity to reach
the older men and women. He told John Wesley that the
Colony would pay for the Indian school if the Moravians would furnish the labor.

The Moravians, a German-speaking people, had fled
to Georgia from Moravia by way of Saxony. With
special permission of the Trustees and under the patron-
age of Count Zinzendorf, they had come in search of
religious freedom and with the hope that a way might
be found for them to preach the gospel to the Indians.
They built a large house in Savannah to which the Indi-
and were welcomed with food and drink. The Indians
showed their appreciation by gifts of grouse and venison. These white people welcomed the opportunity to
practice speaking the red man's language. They were
much pleased with Tomochichi, who had greeted them
and promised to help them in any way he could. As one
of their biographers noted years later, the Moravians felt
that Tomochichi was

> a grave, wise man, resembling one of the old philoso-
> phers, though with him it was natural, not acquired.
> Were he among a hundred Indians, all clothed alike,
> one would point him out and say "that is the king!"[4]

The Moravians were so industrious that in three years they were able to pay off all the money advanced to them. Benjamin Ingham called the Moravians "not only the most useful People in the Colony but also they are certainly the holiest Society of Men in the whole World."[5] It was said also that:

> Many Indians and with them their King, Tomo Tschatchi came to see the brethern and to hear the gospel, or as they expressed it—the great word.[6]

The Moravians petitioned the Trustees to be exempted from carrying arms because it violated their religion, which request was duly granted.

The settlers at Savannah, the Moravians, and the Indians all agreed that a school was needed for their children. When the time came to select a site for it, the Wesley brothers and Moravian Bishop Nitschman were accompanied by Mary Musgrove as they began the search. After examining various tracts of land they finally chose one known as the Irene Mound.[7]

No one knew the origin of the topographical curiosity, but Tomochichi said it was there before his people came. *Irene* meant "Greek messenger of peace." It was a big knoll about 15½ feet in diameter and approximately 160 feet long. A small hill 55 feet by 2½ feet high lay immediately west of the mound, so close that their edges overlapped. Both were located on the western bluff of the Savannah River immediately south of its junction with Pipemakers Creek about 5½ miles above New Yamacraw. During the period when Irene was occupied by the Indians, the area seems to have been entirely surrounded by water except for a narrow section of the river bluff in the southeast portion.

The land was allotted on February 26, 1735, and in August the construction of the school began. The workmen lived with the Indians and Tomochichi took charge of their belongings. The Moravians taught the children the alphabet while working on the structure. The Mico took a lively interest in the project and he, John Wesley and Mary Musgrove visited the building site often. So, too, did the Reverend Benjamin Ingham, who wrote in his diary:

> A door is now Opening for the Conversion of the Indians. There is already a School almost built amongst them. The Indians asked me if I was not afraid to live upon a Hill. I answere'd No. They said the Indians were because they believed that Fairies haunted Hills.[8]

The building was completed by September. It was 60 feet long and 15 feet wide; a room at each end was 15 feet square, with the schoolroom between, and a cellar was dug under one end. The front side faced the rising sun, one end faced due north and the other due south. The new school was dedicated to the Moravians. Peter Rose, his wife, Catherine, and the Reverend Mr. Ingham were the teachers. The Indians gave them five acres of land on which, in addition to their teaching, they were to cultivate a garden so that they would not be dependent on the congregation in Savannah. There were morning and evening readings of the English Bible, as well as prayers. Also one hour each morning, midday, and evening was given to the study of the Indian language. Mrs. Rose taught the girls to read, and the boys who had begun to read she taught to write.

At first everything looked encouraging. Benjamin Ingham, after living several months in the Creek nation, had begun to compile a Creek-English lexicon and grammar. The children learned to read very quickly and some of them could write. They committed many passages to memory and particularly enjoyed singing.

Senauki was very much interested in Irene and the way in which the children were taught. On one visit to the Cowpen Tomochichi and Senauki were accompanied by John Wesley and Benjamin Ingham. The latter recorded in his diary:

> I asked them [the Indians] if they were willing that I should teach the young prince. They consented, desiring me to check and keep him in, but not to strike him.[9]

Tomochichi was much concerned with the school's conduct and prosperity. Chekilli said, as he observed the children studying their lessons, that perhaps the time had come for the Creek children to be educated in the English way, adding:

> White Peoples Children behave themselves like Men,
> we Indians that are Men behave our Selves like dogs.
> Upon all Occasions they are ready to acknowledge
> their Ignorance, which makes me hope they will the
> more readily believe the Mysteries of Christianity.[10]

Malatchi, feeling his importance as a headman, said that
if he had twenty children he would want them all
taught. In a letter to Sir John Phillipps, the Reverend
Mr. Ingham stated,

> The Indians tho at first could hardly be persuaded to
> let one child learn, yet now they are willing to have
> them taught and even Some of the Men Seem to have
> a desire to learn.

The older Indians looked on with wonder and approval. The missionaries had inspired a zeal for master-
ing the English language and took every opportunity to
make the "Great Word" known to the red men. Letters
were written to Tomochichi urging him to fully accept
"the Word."

Rumors of a Spanish war threat began to reach the
colony. Many Indians, unable to resist a war call when
their fighting instincts were aroused, announced that
they were off to protect their English friends from the
Spaniards. Mr. Ingham returned to England to ask for
additional help and teachers for the school, leaving Mr.
Rose in charge. Although the Indians loved the missionary and he was well-meaning, he did not have much

executive ability. The Savannah congregation recalled him and his wife to Savannah to remain until the way opened to send more teachers back to Irene. At about the same time John Wesley returned to England.

The school was left in Moravian hands. On October 7 Anton Seifert and John Böhner moved to New Yamacraw to learn the Creek language and carry on the work of the school. In January 1738 Peter Rose, his wife and daughter returned to Irene. Böhner left to work with the Negroes, and ill health caused Seifert to return to Savannah. The situation became very discouraging. In January 1739 even Peter Rose gave up, moved his family back to the colony and abandoned the school. When Tomachichi died in October, it lost its last friend.

The Moravians' strict rules of living, their daily prayers and religious services, and their refusal to carry arms caused them to become increasingly unpopular with other colonists. Finally leaders of the sect formally petitioned Mr. Causton for permission to quit the colony. They offered to sell their lots and improvements so that they could pay their debts before leaving, but Mr. Causton replied that he could not excuse them without orders from the Trustees. Thus it was that when Benjamin Ingham returned to England to take priest's orders he carried with him a Memorial to that august body.

The Trustees replied that the situation required serious consideration. Since it was the principle of the Moravians not to fight, it should not be required of them. There was reason to suspect that, as Mr. Spangenberg had lately been in Pennsylvania, he may have negotiated with Governor Penn to settle his people under him as their principles were compatible with those of the Quakers. However, the Trustees' reply continued, if they did leave they would either have to pay for their land or forfeit it as they had covenanted to remain upon it three years.[11]

The Moravians were called upon to arm in common defense when the province was threatened with a Spanish invasion. Although the Trustees had granted their petition to be exempt, there was so much ill will expressed toward them that in 1738 a portion of the group migrated to Pennsylvania to join the Reverend August Gottlieb Spangenberg, their leader, who had left Savannah previously. When those remaining were again urged to bear arms in 1739, they left to join their friends in Pennsylvania. Thus ended the first mission of the United Brethren in America.[12]

While in England Oglethorpe had urged the preparation of a simple manual which he might have translated into the Indian language. The finished book was dedicated to the Trustees and printed at the expense of the Society for the Propagation of the Gospel. It was published in 1740 and by 1764 was in its 10th edition, with a French translation having been made. "This style breathes so strongly of the spirit of primitive piety, its style is so clear, its plan so easy for minds even the most limited—it is a true representation of . . . religion," Mr. Oglethorpe wrote in a letter from Fort Frederica in 1741.

By then, however, it was too late. Irene had been abandoned and Tomochichi's dream of educating his people had faded away.

9

THE SPANISH THREAT

In 1734, while Tomochichi was in England, Spanish and Yamasee warriers had attacked a Yamacraw hunting party and killed Umpechi's brother. Licka, an anti-Spanish headman, desired vengeance on the Spaniards for killing his brother and drinking wine from his skull. He said that to prevent the Creeks from going to St. Augustine for presents, the path must be made bloody. Patrick McKay, Georgia Indian agent, discreetly told Licka that the English could not take sides in this quarrel but that he ought to follow the dictates of his heart.[1] McKay's interpreter, checked by no such scruples, told Licka the English would welcome Spanish blood.[2] Licka took a war party to Florida and killed a Spaniard and several Yamasees. When Spanish protests were made in Carolina and Georgia and at the English

Court, English officials denounced the act. In June
1735, when Licka appeared at the Savannah Conference
for the distribution of presents, Georgia authorities were
much embarrassed. Licka, of course, should be rewarded
for effecting a break in Spanish-Creek relations, but to
do so officially would cause international complications.
The Georgians ostentatiously ignored him, but gave gifts
to other headmen who saw that Licka got his share.[3]

Tomochichi, who missed his friend very much, retained two Indian runners to bring him news of Oglethorpe's return to Georgia. Barely had the White Chief
arrived on the ship "Simmonds, on February 6, 1736,
when the Mico with forty warriots appeared. "I've come
to stake out limits of our territories," he told his friend,
"then we'll return to the mainland and hunt."

Some neighboring Carolinians attempted to preju-
dice the Indians against Mr. Oglethorpe and the Georgia
Colony. This might have had very serious consequences
had not Tomochichi remained firm in his interest and
friendship. However, the stories told by the Carolinians
caused only forty of a promised two hundred Indians to
accompany Mr. Oglethorpe to St. Simons Island.[4]

In May the forty warriors and hunters set out in
canoes, followed by Mr. Oglethorpe, the Mico, and
Toonahowi. Their objective was to designate the precise
boundaries dividing the lands ceded by the Creeks to the
Colony from those of the Spaniards. The Indians also
wished to spy out the Spanish positions and to achieve
vengeance for the killing of Umpechi's brother and
other Yamacraws. They passed St. Simons, Jekyll,

which had already been explored, and the Missoe or Sassafras Island which lay just beyond. Toonahowi asked that the name of the last island be changed to Cumberland Island after the Duke of Cumberland who had given him a gold watch. Below St. George's Island the Chief and Indians reported there were campfires and unidentified white men. The old Mico, hatred for the Spanish written on his face, wanted to attack the enemy immediately. Oglethorpe, being uncertain what to do, refused. There were strong words exchanged--perhaps the strongest ever passed between the White Leader and his Indian ally.

"You want to kill your enemies by night because you fear them by day!" challenged Oglethorpe.

"That's not so," replied the Chief. "If you don't kill them tonight, they'll kill you tomorrow!"

No attacks were made. Daylight showed that the "enemy" was an English party returning from Florida. Oglethorpe requested that the Indians avoid conflict with the Spaniards and that they be on the lookout for unfriendly soldiers.

The reconnaissance group proceeded southward so that the Mico could point out the southern boundaries of the ceded Indian lands. Mr. Oglethorpe decided that the south branch of the Altamaha River passed St. Simons and Jekyll Islands. Therefore, he added those two islands to the territory of the Georgia Colony. When the party reached the St. Mary's River, the White Chief concluded that possibly it flowed northwestward and was the south branch of the Altamaha. This decision permitted him to include the remaining sea islands of Cumberland and Amelia in the Trustees' Colony.

The party returned to Frederica, where the Indians gave a lively war dance. Then, fearing another Spanish attack, messengers were sent to call down more Creek warriors. No attack was made.[5] Tomochichi returned to Savannah with sixty Indians to assist in building the fort at Savannah,[6] to rest, and to take care of the wants of his family and tribe.

Oglethorpe had gained permission to build forts as a protection to the Colony. He had already selected a site which was located on the west side of St. Simons Island for which he had chosen the name "Fort Frederica" in honor of Frederick, Prince of Wales, eldest son of King George. This settlement, which he planned, became the pride of his heart. It was located on a bluff on the western side of the island along the inland channel, looking out toward the wide mouth of the Altamaha River. He built a simple frame cottage, "Orange Hall," the only real home he ever had in Georgia.[7] This typically English house, surrounded by a garden and an orchard of figs and grapes, was shaded by massive oaks which protected it from the hot sun. The sea breezes cooled the atmosphere and the fragrance of wild flowers permeated the air. During the summer months when he was in residence there, Oglethorpe returned to Savannah by boat at intervals to take care of official matters.

The Scottish Highlanders, who had come over to join the Colony, settled at New Inverness, near the present town of Darien. When they were warned that being so close to the Spanish might cause them to be massacred, they laughed and said they did not intend to be frightened. Nevertheless, when Oglethorpe arrived unannounced, the Scotsmen armed themselves and would not permit him to enter until he had identified himself, which pleased the visitor very much. On subsequent visits he often wore their costume with its plaid kilt and cap.

Fort Howe was established ten miles from New Inverness on the Altamaha River to command its fords; Fort Argyle was located on the Ogeechee River where the Indian trail crossed it, and below New Inverness, on the mainland, was the outpost Carteret. In order to connect New Inverness with Savannah, Oglethorpe decided to build a coastal highway. Captain Hugh Mackay, Jr. with a company of Rangers was sent to compute the distance and select the most practical route between the two settlements. Tomochichi's guides blazed the trail which ran through marshes and dense jungle. This was the first road constructed in the colony. Later called the Savannah Coastal Highway and now known as the Ogeechee Road, it is still in use. The Savannah Chapter of the Daughters of the American Revolution has posted an historical marker in Savannah's Madison Square to commemorate the opening of the road.

Once more Oglethorpe returned to England, this time aboard the "Twin Brothers," on November 23. 1736. He was faced with many problems. The establishment of the new posts had been very expensive. In desperation, the Trustees had passed along the bills to Parliament. His personal resources were sadly depleted in the cause of Georgia. On March 9, 1734 he had explained to South Carolina his financial inability to create more frontier garrisons for their protection, explaining that at present he was so limited that he "could not go into any expenses farther than making Presents to the Indians, wherewith to assure their firm attachment to the English cause."

Mr. Oglethorpe petitioned Parliament for £30,000 toward the expense of the Colony and the support of a company of Rangers for its protection. He reminded the Assembly that he had gone overseas, venturing his life and health to the neglect of his own affairs and had already spent £3,000 of his own money. When Parliament protested the amount of money, arguing that Great Britain had already spent more money on Georgia than on any of its other colonies, Oglethorpe instructed Verelst to raise all the money he could from the commander's real and personal estate and to use his salary from the Government to help meet the bills. Then Oglethorpe personally supplied the money. By March 1744 Oglethorpe had spent £91,705 13s 5d[8] of his own resources. Although Parliament authorized that he be repaid on March 20, there is some doubt that he actually was reimbursed.

Back in America, South Carolina was angry because the Indian trade must be licensed through Savannah, a procedure which deprived Charles Town of profitable business. Spain complained about the proximity of the new settlement at Frederica. The Trustees were annoyed because they were not given more regular reports. The Indians were angry with the English because their people were almost destroyed by rum and small pox carried into their nation by the white traders, claiming that over one thousand of them had died and that the sickness raged so severely that they were unable to cultivate their fields. Because their Leader was forced to spend so much time in the southern settlements, problems began to accumulate in Savannah and the malcontents began complaining to the Trustees.

In June 1737 Oglethorpe was appointed general of the forces of South Carolina and Georgia.[9] In September he was made colonel of a regiment in England to be raised for the defense of Georgia. The regiment was mustered into service in a short time, officered by gentlemen of character and importance. Attached to it were twenty cadets who later were promoted as vacancies occurred, and in addition forty more men were taken along at the Colonel's expense. Each man was allowed to take a wife for whom food and extra pay were provided. As soon as part of the regiment was organized and drilled, he sent it to the fort at Frederica. The new general now had at his command a full and well-appointed regiment.

General Oglethorpe's main concern was to get more military help for Georgia. Once more he successfully appeased the Trustees with honeyed words and won their support with a more equable balance sheet, a Carolina compromise, and malcontent silence, but the

Spanish issue remained.

The General arrived at St. Simons on September 18, 1738 with a regiment of seven hundred men. On October 8 he set out for Savannah in an open boat accompanied by two other boats. He was greeted upon his arrival by all the magistrates and saluted by cannon and militia; the people spent the night making big bonfires and rejoicing. The next day Tomochichi arrived. When the Englishman looked into the drawn, worn face of the Mico who was still recovering from a long illness, the aged Indian straightened his bent shoulders and said, "seeing the great man restores me, makes me 'moult like and eagle'."[10] He explained that the chiefs of several towns were waiting to welcome him and to assure him of their fidelity to the King.

The Governor of Florida invited several Creek chiefs to St. Augustine to greet Oglethorpe, whom he said was visiting there. The Indians soon realized it was a hoax and that they had been summoned to hear anti-English talk.[11] They downed their rum, swept up the presents and went off to Savannah to reaffirm their loyalty to the English.

In October Tomochichi brought the King of the Chehaws, Mico Oakmugee, with thirty warriors and fifty-two attendants to a reception for General Oglethorpe. They assured the White Chief that the remaining towns would be informed of his return and would be prepared to send one thousand warriors to any point he should designate, being subject to his command. They invited the General to visit their towns. Handsome presents were distributed to the red men. That night they had a dance which the Leader attended.

"I need your help," confessed Oglethorpe to his friend Tomochichi.

"I am too old now and can only be your advisor," the Mico replied, "but these men, one thousand Creek warriors, are ready and willing to serve you, to go where you command." The General realized then that his red friends were more loyal to him than were many of the white men.

War between Spain and England threatened. Oglethorpe realized this and directed his full attention to the matter. The French and Spanish cooperated in an attempt to separate the Creeks from the English. Tomochichi had supplied many guides to the white men; now he furnished warriors who went on military expeditions. When it was rumored that there were strange Indians in the region, the Mico, being involved in matters which demanded his presence at New Yamacraw, sent warriors to investigate, telling them that although he was unable to accompany them, if they encountered any trouble they were to send for him immediately and nothing would keep him from joining his men. Three of the Indians who had gone to England accompanied the scouts, taking Mary Musgrove as their interpreter. The red men showed caution and courage.

It was vital to keep the Indians on England's side against the Spanish. A massive attack from Havanna against the Colony was being planned by the Spanish.[12] Their emissaries were trying to incite an insurrection

among the South Carolina slaves and were attempting to
recruit Indians at Coweta. General Oglethorpe wrote the
Trustees that Chief Chekilli and Chief Malachee insisted
that he come to put things in order. He had been told
that all the chiefs of the Nation were to come to Coweta
to meet him and to hold a general council. The enmity
or friendship of seven thousand warriors was at stake.

The General went to Tomochichi for advice. The
Mico encouraged him to meet with the Indians at their
great Council at Coweta. He told the Englishman not to
take along a company of soldiers as if needing protection but to go alone except for a small escort of guides,
then the Indians would know that he came as a friend,
confident, unafraid and seeking peaceful relations with
the red men. So on July 17, 1739 the White Leader set
out with his servants, three men, and Mary Mathews;
they were joined en route by a small party of rangers
and Indian guides.

Coweta Town, located more than four hundred
miles inland in what later became northwest Georgia,
could be reached only by following rivers and trails,
fording streams, cutting through underbrush, and moving cautiously through swamps and deep forests. Each
day's travel took the party deeper into the lands of
Indians whose loyalty the Spanish were trying to buy.
The wilderness made them extremely vulnerable to
ambush and for awhile they thought they were being
shadowed by Spanish horsemen, but there was no attack at any time during the three-week march. Instead,
as they approached their destination, they found cakes

OGLETHORPE TRAVELS TO COWETA TOWN

and bags of flour had been set out for their use. They were met near Chattahoochee, forty miles from Coweta, by Indian boys and girls who gave them watermelons, muscadines, venison and wild turkey meat. From there an escort accompanied them on the remainder of the journey.

The great assembly of Creeks, Chickasaws, Choctaws, Cherokees, and other tribes of the great Muskogean family convened on August 11 and continued for ten days with great ceremony. General Oglethorpe sat with the Indians on logs covered with bearskins, drank their black tea and smoked the peace pipe with them. The Indians called him *Tasanagi—Takke*—White Chief.

The treaty which was concluded at Coweta on August 21, 1739 was an important event in the annals of the southern frontier. The Creeks repledged their loyalty to George II and confirmed the grants of land they had made six years before. The General promised to give the Indians 15,000 bushels of corn to feed their hungry people. At this news the red men whooped so loudly that they almost deafened their white guests. The Englishman also promised to continue to observe the boundaries of the territories reserved by the Indians for their own use. Inaccurate weights and measures used in trading were to be investigated. White traders were to be instructed to deal more honestly with the red men and were not to trespass on Indian land.

General Oglethorpe felt that his journey had been worthwhile. On the trip back to Savannah he fell from his horse into a canebrake and a sharp cane pierced his side. The wound became infected. The Englishman remained in Augusta for several weeks, ill with fever and malaria, where he found bed rest and proper food for recovery. While there he received a message from William Stephens telling him that Spain had declared war on England. He left his bed and lost no time hurrying down the river to Savannah, which he reached on September 22, 1739.[13]

10

DEATH OF TOMOCHICHI

Soon after Oglethorpe arrived in Savannah he learned that Tomochichi was gravely ill. He set out immediately for New Yamacraw in the hope of comforting his great and good friend.

The ninety-seven-year-old[1] Mico, who had until then been active and vigorous, lay ill many days. As his strength ebbed he was visited by many of his English friends as well as by his own sorrowing people.

The Reverend John Wesley visited him and was deeply moved at the sight of the prostrate chieftain, whose wife Senauki slowly fanned her husband with a bunch of feathers.[2] When Wesley returned to Savannah he noted in his journal that he was "ill with grief."

Another visitor, the Reverend George Whitefield, later recorded the events of his trips to see the Mico.

I went to see Tomo Chachi, who I heard was near expiring at a Neighbour's House. He lay on a Blanket, thin and meagure, and little else but Skin and Bones. Senauki sat by fanning him with some Indian Feathers. There was no body that could talk English, so I could only shake Hands and leave.

[Later:]

Went once more to see Tomo Chachi hearing his nephew Toonoowee was there who could talk English. I desired him to inquire of his Uncle Wether he thought he should die.

I can not tell, replied Tomochichi.

Where do you think you will go after Death? To Heaven, the Mico replied.

I then asked Whether he believed in Heaven? He answered, Yes.

I then asked Whether he believed a Hell? and described it by pointing to a Fire.

He replied, No From whence we may easily gather, how natural it is to all Mankind to believe there is a Place of Happiness, because they wish it may be so, and on the contrary, how averse they are to believe a Place of Torment, because they wish it may not be so. But God is true and just, and as surely as the Good shall go into everlasting Happiness, so the Wicked shall go into everlasting Punishment.[3]

The Chief, when warned that death was near, showed no fear. Propped up against the trunk of a live oak tree, he urged his people "never to forget the favors he had received from the King when in England but to preserve their Friendship with the English."[4] He expressed great fondness for James Oglethorpe. His only regret regarding his life was that he should die at a time when he might have been useful against the Spanish.

"Bury me," he requested, "in the white men's town, in the land which my people gave them and in the home which I helped them build."

As General Oglethorpe neared New Yamacraw, the great Tomochichi quietly expired on October 5, 1737. The grief-striken White Chief decreed that his friend should be honored with a public military funeral such as the people of Savannah had never seen before.[5]

Late on the afternoon of October 10, as sunlight filtered through the heavy foliage of the tall moss-draped oaks, Tomochichi's body was brought down by water. His long thin figure, wrapped in blankets, lay on a litter which took up almost the full length of the boat. General Oglethorpe, the magistrates and the people of the Colony met it at the edge of the water.

The bier was supported by General Oglethorpe, his head bowed and his eyes clouded, who led the funeral procession, followed by Colonel Stephens, Colonel Montaigut, Mr. Carteret, Mr. Lemon and Mr. Maxwell; next an armed escort of forty freeholders; and then a solemn parade of the members of the community and Indians. They marched to Percival Square, where the grave site was placed exactly in the center of the park.[6] According to Indian custom, there was no religious

ceremony.[7] Minute guns were fired fired from the Ba-
tery all during the burial. Seven minute guns were dis-
charged and forth men in arms gave three volleys over
the grave after the body was lowered into the ground.
Then Senauki, very thin, old, and bent with grief, and
Toonahowi, now grown to full manhood, walked up to
the excavation and sadly tossed Tomochichi's blanket,
headdress, beads, arrows, and a few pieces of silver into
the grave.

James Oglethorpe ordered that a pyramid of stones
dug in the neighborhood be erected over the grave as an
ornament and as a testimony of Savannah's gratitude
and admiration for this great man.[8] It was Indian custom to bury a chief under a mound. This monument
would represent a mound to the Indians and a cairn to
the English.

The respect and honor paid their Mico gave the
Indians great satisfaction and helped preserve the friendship and loyalty this venerable Indian had so successfully spent his last years creating.

To the day of his death Tomochichi had kept his
pledge of amity and the assurances of good will given
during his first interview with James Oglethorpe. He had
repeatedly proved himself the firm friend of the white
man, the guide, adviser and protector of the colonists,
the constant companion and faithful confederate of
Oglethorpe.[9]

Faithful as an ally, generous as a friend, active and
efficient as a warrior, Tomochichi merits the praise and
respect of all Georgians.[10]

TOMOCHICHI'S GRAVE IN WRIGHT SQUARE
This old stereoptican view of what was originally Percival Square clearly depicts the Mico's
final resting place. *From the DeRenne Collection
in the Ilah Dunlap Little Library at the University
of Georgia, Athens.*

11

EPILOGUE

Immediately after Tomochichi's burial General Oglethorpe sent Indians speeding to the tribes to summon warriors and dispatched Mary Mathews to rouse the chiefs to the aid of Georgia. England was at war with Spain!

Toonahowi, in charge of an Indian legion, distinguished himself in battle. He shot a Spanish captain in the head in a hand-to-hand encounter. In 1743 his outfit ambushed a party of Spanish horsemen near St. Augustine. Toonahowi was killed[1]—the only fatality in one of the most successful English exploits in Florida. The Mico would have been proud of his dearly beloved heir who followed the example of his uncle, the great Indian King, so faithfully and selflessly.

Unfortunately, the Mico would not have experienced the same pride in the activities of the former Princess Coosaponekeesa. Mary Musgrove Mathews became increasingly a source of trouble for the Colony of Georgia. She married as her third husband the Reverend Thomas Bosomworth, who had been chaplain of Oglethorpe's regiment. Under the guidance of this avaricious and unscrupulous man, Mary was persuaded to lay claim to the sea islands of St. Catherine's, Ossabaw, and Sapelo and to proclaim herself an Indian empress. Besieged by his creditors in South Carolina, Bosomworth prevailed upon his wife to make a claim upon the costly items which the King had recently sent over as presents to the Indians. There followed a series of intrigues so outrageous as to excite disbelief, and before the final curtain was rung down on her activities this woman who once had been so good a friend to the colonists was revealed to them and to the Indians as a double-dealing trouble-maker who put self-interest above everything else.

Although Mary had been deeded the land upon which Tomochichi had built New Yamacraw, the title was not upheld by the Colony and, therefore, ownership reverted to the Crown. The population of the village declined gradually over a period of many years after the Mico's death, even though its inhabitants were free of both taxes and land rent.

A century and a half later the site of New Yamacraw had returned to its original natural state. Although the Yamasee Nation and its language both became

Georgia Historical Society

THE BOSOMWORTHS PRESENT THEIR DEMANDS

extinct, the blood lines of that proud people probably are perpetuated even today by the Seminole and Creek tribes into which the last Yamasees were absorbed.[2] As the old Yamasee lands passed into possession of the white man,[3] the important role played by the former owners became a remote memory.

Let none forget, however, that the modern
Georgian owes much to the red men who once occupied
that portion of present-day Savannah which is west of
Jefferson Street. Georgia's oldest and, some say, its
most beautiful city abounds with historical reminders of
the great events which occurred in the years after 1733.
There have been many changes in the nearly two-and-a-
half centuries since that auspicious year, but in Savannah tradition and history are cherished as in few other
places.

The name of Percival Square, which had honored
Trustee John Viscount Percival, later the Earl of
Egmont, was changed to Wright Square in 1764 in
honor of Sir James Wright, the last of the royal gover-
nors of Georgia. No attempt was ever made to disturb
Tomochichi's remains.

A newspaper article in 1878 stated that a frame
residence on lot 133 York Street near Bull Street had
been removed. In excavating, a human skeleton had
been found four feet below the surface along with several rusty and corroded coffin nails, pieces of iron
shaped like the blade of a hatchet, and a piece of ivory.
The lot was part of Percival Square. The building had
been standing for over seventy years, probably the first
structure erected after the Square had been divided into
lots. It was suggested that these might have been the remains of Tomochichi.[4]

This could not have been true. The Colonial Ceme-
tery had originally occupied the site of the two York
lots, Trust lots R, on the southwest corner of Bull

Street.[5] In 1755 permission was granted to use the two
lots for a school.[6] In 1759 it was decided to use one lot
for the school and sell the second lot. Therefore, it was
not surprising that skeletal remains from the old burying
site were found when the lot was excavated in 1878.[7]

John De Brahm, an engineer, in his *History of the
Province of Georgia* dated 1752 shows a plan of the City
of Savannah which marks "Tomochichi's Tomb" with a
small square in the exact center of Percival Square. The
streets, as originally planned, were all laid out at that
time and were not thereafter changed. Therefore, the
Mico's body could not have been found so far from its
original place of interment.

Many years later few citizens knew why a pyramid
of stones stood in the center of one of the principal
squares. Children danced around the pile of rocks and
sang:

> *Old Tom O Chi Chi,*
> *What are you doing tonight,*
> *Doing tonight,*
> *Doing tonight.*

not knowing who invented the game or why.

There has been controversy concerning the exact
location of Tomochichi's grave and uncertainty as to
whether a marker had been placed over it. Colonel
Stephens noted in his Journal on October 6, 1739 that
the Government "intends to place an obelisk or the
like over Tomochichi's grave as an ornament to the

town and a memorial to the Indians." *The Gentleman's Magazine*, London, October 10, 1739, noted that Oglethorpe had ordered a "Pyramid of Stone" which was to be dug up in the neighborhood and was to be erected in the center of the town as a testimony of gratitude.

The square which John de Brahm used to indicate Tomochichi's grave suggests that it was a pyramid. On September 18, 1759, "His Excellency proposed to the Board that the Public Market intended to be built around the public pump should be removed to Tomochichi's burial place. . . . Resolved by his Excellency in Council to build a Market House around Thomoe Chichi's burying ground 60 feet square consisting of four buildings twelve feet square each, the interspaces to be covered with a Shed of the same Breadth supported in the center by Cedar Posts."[8] This implies that there was to be a central courtyard surrounding the grave.

Hill's painting of Savannah in 1855 pictures a pyramid, a high mound topped with an ornamental cast iron urn.[9] So there is historical evidence to support the tradition that a marker was placed over Tomochichi's burial place.

William Harden (1844–1936), Georgia Historical Society librarian for seventy years, stated four years before his death that from earliest childhood he remembered a high vine-covered rocky earth mound which had been pointed out to him by his father and several aged inhabitants of Savannah as Tomochichi's grave and that it was there, in the center of Wright Square, until 1882.

In December of that year the earth mound was removed in preparation for the erection of an imposing monument in memory of William Washington Gordon, founder and first president of the Central of Georgia Railroad. Mr. Harden was there and watched the activity. He said no excavation was done to prepare the foundation for the Gordon monument; only the surface ground was pounded down. So it can only be assumed that Tomochichi's remains rest today where they were placed by the Georgia colonists so many years ago.

Late in the 1880s the Georgia Society of the Colonial Dames of America decided that the memory of the great Indian Chief who had contributed so much to the survival of Savannah deserved lasting tribute.[10] Mrs. W. W. Gordon II, daughter-in-law of the man in whose memory the monument had been erected on the site of the Mico's burial place, wrote to the Stone Mountain Company in Atlanta inquiring the price of a large boulder of Georgia granite which might serve as a monument.

The company replied that it had a granite boulder, the world's largest monolith, which it would be delighted to send as a gift to the Colonial Dames; as General Gordon had been president of the railroad, there would be no freight charge.

"The Ladies wish it to be our gift. We would like a bill," replied Mrs. Gordon. Subsequently a bill for the sum of one dollar "payable on the Day of Judgment" was received and duly paid.

The tremendous granite boulder was placed in the southeast section of Wright Square. It was dedicated to the memory of Tomochichi on April 21, 1899.

On the face of the boulder is a large copper plate encircled by arrow heads and Cherokee roses. A tomahawk and a peace pipe balance the coat of arms of the Colonial Dames.

The inscription reads:

> *In memory of Tomo-chi-chi*
> *The Mico of the Yamacraws*
> *The companion of Oglethorpe*
> *And the Friend and Ally of the*
> *Colony of Georgia*

SOURCE NOTES

Chapter 1
TOMOCHICHI'S PEOPLE

1. *Dictionary of American Biography* (New York: 1936–64) IX: 580.

2. Paul S. Martin, *Indians before Columbus* (Chicago: 1947), 360.

3. Albert Samuel Gatschet, *A Migration Legend of the Creek Indians* (AMS Press: 1884–1888), I: 58–59. There are various spellings of the name. Maskóki, Maskógi, Maskóki designates a single person of the Creek tribe. Collective plural is Maskokalgi. The English authors write this name Muscogee, Muskhogee, and its plural Muscogulgee. Other spellings will also be found.

4. Frederick Webb Hodge, *Handbook of American Indians North of Mexico* (Washington: 1907–10), I: 961.

5. William Bacon Stevens, *History of Georgia* (Savannah: 1972), I: 51.

6. Gatschet, *Migration Legend*, Pt. III: 153.

7. *Ibid.*, I: 10, 154–156.

8. Stevens, *History of Georgia*, I: 51.

9. Gatschet, *Migration Legend*, I: 236–251; John Reed Swanton, *Social Organization and Social Usages of the Indians of the Creek Confederacy* (Washington: 1924–25, XLII: 34–38; "Some Ancient Georgia Indian Lore," *Georgia Historical Quarterly*, Notes & Documents 15 (2): 192–201, June 1931 (Athens: 1931), 192–193; Fullham Mss. Virginia 2nd Box No. 131 (copy of original is in Georgia Historical Society Library, Savannah).

10. Stevens, *History of Georgia*, I: 51–52.

11. John Reed Swanton, *Indian Tribes of North America* (Washington: 1952), 104.

12. John Reed Swanton, *Early History of the Creek Indians and Their Neighbors* (Washington: 1922), 132–133.

13. Hodge, *Handbook*, I: 363.

14. "Final Report of the United States DeSoto Commission," *House Document 71*, 76th Congress, 1st Session (Washington: 1939), 49.

15. Edward Gaylord Bourne, *Narratives of the Career of Hernando de Soto* (New York: 1904), I: 65–66.

16. *Ibid.*, I: 66.

17. Lawton Bryan Evans, *First Lessons in Georgia History* (New York: 1913), 17–18.

18. Bourne, *Narratives*, I: 71.

19. Herbert Ravenel Sass, *The Story of the South Carolina Low Country* (West Columbia: n.d.), I: 32.

20. James Etheridge Callaway, *The Early Settlement of Georgia* (Athens: 1948), 13. Allen Daniel Candler, *The Colonial Records of the State of Georgia* (Atlanta: 1904–16), VI: 148.

21. Stevens, *History of Georgia*, I: 52.

22. Hodge, *Handbook*, II: 776.

23. *Ibid.*, I: 551.

24. *Ibid.*, I: 551.

25. Walter A. Harris, *Here the Creeks Sat Down* (Macon: 1958), 15.

26. Hodge, *Handbook*, I: 68.

27. Bernice McCullar, *This Is Your Georgia* (Northport: 1966), 82.

28. John Tate Lanning, *Spanish Missions of Georgia* (Chapel Hill: 1935), 10.

29. Swanton, *Indian Tribes*, 114.

30. Swanton, *Early History of the Creek Indians*, 95.

31. Swanton, *Indian Tribes*, 114.

32. Delores Floyd, "Legend of Sir Walter Raleigh at Savannah," *Georgia Historical Quarterly* 23 (2): 103-121, June 1939 (Athens: 1939), 104; Charles Colcock Jones, Jr., *Antiquities of the Southern Indians* (New York: 1873), 131.

Chapter 2
HUNTER AND WARRIOR

1. *Gentleman's Magazine* (London: 1740), X: 129.

2. John Reed Swanton, *Indians of the Southeastern United States* (Washington: 1946), 208.

3. John Reed Swanton, *Early History of the Creek Indians and Their Neighbors* (Washington: 1922), 108.

4. *Ibid.*, 96.

5. Stevens, *History of Georgia*, I: 46.

6. Swanton, *Early History of the Creek Indians*, 10?

7. Chapman J. Milling, *Red Carolinians* (Chapel '1940), 177; *Indian Book* Journal of the Cherokee Trade (⌐ ton: 18th cent.), I, Pt. I: 48.

8. Herbert Ravenel Sass, *The Story of the South Carolina Low Country* (West Columbia: n.d.), I: 49.

9. *Ibid.*, I: 32-37; Ruth Suddeth, *Empire Builders of Georgia* (Austin: 1951), 24-25; Thomas L. Stokes, *The Savannah* (New York: 1951), 32-49, 89.

10. *Gentleman's Magazine*, 1740, X: 129.

11. Walter A. Harris, *Here the Creeks Sat Down* (Macon: 1958), 51; Verner Winslow Crane, *The Southern Frontier 1670-1732* (Ann Arbor: 1929), 83.

12. David H. Corkran, *The Creek Frontier 1540-1783* (Norman: 1967), 56.

13. Edwin Green, *Indians of South Carolina* (Columbia: 1920), 71-72.

14. Harris, *Here the Creeks Sat Down*, 51. Brim's Indian name "The name of Hoboyetly, King of the Cowetas," appears first among signatures to the alliance "A Humble Submission to the Crown of England"; Sass, *South Carolina Low Country*, I: 35. Yslachamuque Indian name of Brim-Gran Cazique of the Apalachicoles (later to be called Creeks) known to English as Brims.

15. Milling, *Red Carolinians*, 178.

16. Swanton, *Early History of the Creek Indians*, 101.

17. Harris, *Here the Creeks Sat Down*, 53.

18. Corkran, *Creek Frontier*, 63.

19. *Colonial Records of South Carolina*, "Journal of the Commons House of Assembly, Nov. 10, 1736-June 7, 1739" (Columbia: 1951), I: 108.

20. Allen Daniel Candler, *The Colonial Records of the State of Georgia* (Atlanta: 1904-1916), XXXVI: 316.

21. Corkran, *Creek Frontier*, 83.

22. *Ibid.*, 79.

Chapter 3

TOMOCHICHI AND OGLETHORPE

1. Henry Bruce, *Life of Oglethorpe* (New York: 1890), 112.

2. Charles Colcock Jones, Jr., *Historical Sketch of Tomochichi* (Albany: 1868), 18–19.

3. Bruce, *Life of Oglethorpe*, 112.

4. *Colonial Records of South Carolina*, "Journal of the Commons House of Assembly Nov. 10, 1736–June 7, 1739" (Columbia: 1951), I: 153–154.

5. *Dictionary of American Biography* (New York: 1936–64), VII, Pt. 2: 1.

6. William Bacon Stevens, *History of Georgia* (Savannah: 1972), I: 476–493, Charter of the Colony of Georgia, I: 463–475, List of Trustees.

7. Thomas Gamble, "Colonel William Bull—His Part in the Founding of Savannah," *Georgia Historical Quarterly* XVII (2): 111–126, June 1933 (Athens: 1933), 114.

8. Mills Lane, ed., *General Oglethorpe's Georgia; Colonial Letters, 1733–43* (Savannah: 1975), I: 4.

9. E. Merton Coulter, ed., *The Journal of Peter Gordon 1732–1735* (Athens: 1963), 35.

10. Gamble, "Colonel William Bull," 115; Edward McGrady, *The History of South Carolina Under the Royal Government 1719-1776* (New York: 1899), 164.

11. Allen Daniel Candler, *The Colonial Records of the State of Georgia* (Atlanta: 1904–16), III: 380; Lane, *General Oglethorpe's Georgia*, 1, 5; Amos A. Ettinger, *James Edward Oglethorpe* (Oxford: 1936), 111-112.

12. Candler, *Colonial Records of Georgia*, III: 381 (Oglethorpe to the Trustees 2/20/1733); Amos Ettinger, *James Edward Oglethorpe* (Oxford: 1936), 133.

13. Stevens, *History of Georgia*, I: 89.

14. Charles Colcock Jones, Jr., *History of Georgia* (Boston: 1883), I: 119–120; Stevens, *History of Georgia*, I: 229.

15. Jones, *History of Georgia*, I: 135–136.

16. *Ibid.*, I: 135.

Chapter 4

THE GEORGIA COLONY

1. E. Merton Coulter, ed., *The Journal of Peter Gordon 1732–1735* (Athens, 1963), 35–36.

2. *Ibid.*, 36.

3. *Ibid.*, 43.

4. Charles Colcock Jones, Jr., *Historical Sketch of Tomochichi* (Albany: 1868), 30, Note 1.

5. Coulter, *The Journal of Peter Gordon*, 45.

6. *Ibid.*, 37.

7. Louis DeVorsey, Jr., "Indian Boundaries in Colonial Georgia," *Georgia Historical Quarterly* LIV Spring 1970: 63–78 (Athens: 1970), 65; Allen Daniel Candler, *The Colonial Records of the State of Georgia* (Atlanta: 1904–16), I: 31; Thomas Gamble, "Colonel William Bull—His Part in the Founding of Savannah," *Georgia Historical Quarterly* XVII (2): 111–126 June 1933 (Athens: 1933), 113–114.

8. Charles Colcock Jones, Jr., *History of Georgia* (Boston: 1883), I: 137.

9. Henry Bruce, *Life of Oglethorpe* (New York: 1890), 112-113.

10. Jones, *History of Georgia*, 139.

11. John Tate Lanning, *Spanish Missions of Georgia* (Chapel Hill: 1935), 11.

12. Jones, *Historical Sketch of Tomochichi*, 31.

13. *Ibid.*, 36.

14. Jones, *Historical Sketch of Tomochichi*, 33-36, text of Articles of Friendship & Commerce.

15. Candler, *Colonial Records of Georgia*, XXI: 196; Amos A. Ettinger, *James Edward Oglethorpe* (Oxford: 1936), 182.

16. Latter citation, 181-182.

17. Bruce, *Life of Oglethorpe*, 119; Jones, *Historical Sketch of Tomochichi*, 55; *Monthly Intelligencer* (London: 1734), 449.

18. Samuel Urlsperger, ed., *Detailed Reports on the Salzburger Emigrants Who Settled in America* (Athens: 1968), I: 145.

19. Thaddeus Harris, *Biographical Memorials of James Oglethorpe, Founder of the Colony of Georgia in North America* (Boston: 1841), 360.

20. *Savannah Morning News* Nov. 24, 1963, Magazine Section, p. 5; *Savannah Georgian*, May 1, 1828, p. 2, col. 1.

21. Baron George Philipp Von Reck, "Commissary Von Reck's Report on Georgia," *Georgia Historical Quarterly* 47 (1): 95-110 March 1963 (Athens: 1963), 106.

22. Jones, *Historical Sketch of Tomochichi*, 54.

Chapter 5

TOMOCHICHI IN ENGLAND

1. William Bacon Stevens, *History of Georgia* (Savannah: 1972), I: 117.

2. Amos A. Ettinger, *James Edward Oglethorpe* (Oxford: 1936), 144.

3. David H. Corkran, *The Creek Frontier 1540–1783* (Norman: 1967), 85. *Gentleman's Magazine* (London: 1734), IV: 329.

4. *London Magazine* (London: 1734), III, 384.

5. Samuel Urlsperger, ed., *Detailed Reports on the Salzburger Emigrants Who Settled in America* (Athens: 1968), I: 19.

6. *London Daily Journal* June 19–20, 1734.

7. Charles Colcock Jones, Jr., *Historical Sketch of Tomochichi* (Albany: 1868), 60.

8. *London Journal*, June 22 and 29, 1734.

9. Robert G. McPherson, ed., *The Journal of the Earl of Egmont 1732–1738* (Athens: 1962), p. 65.

10. *Ibid.*, 58; Candler, *Colonial Records of Georgia*, I: 177–178.

11. *Journal of the Earl of Egmont*, p. 69.

12. *Monthly Intelligencer* (London: 1734), August 17, 1734, p. 450.

13. *Journal of the Earl of Egmont*, p. 61.

14. *Ibid.*, 62.

15. Stevens, *History of Georgia*, 120; *Gentleman's Magazine*, XIV: 449.

16. Henry Bruce, *Life of Oglethorpe* (New York: 1890), p. 146.

17. *Journal of the Earl of Egmont*, p. 61.

18. Jones, *Historical Sketch of Tomochichi*, 67–68.

19. *Journal of the Earl of Egmont*, p. 59.

20. Charles Colcock Jones, Jr., *Antiquities of the Southern Indians* (New York: 1873), 185–186.

21. Candler, *Colonial Records of Georgia*, II: 73.

22. *Journal of the Earl of Egmont*, p. 62.

23. Charles Colcock Jones, Jr., *History of Georgia* (Boston: 1883), I: 183.

24. Candler, *Colonial Records of Georgia*, XXIX: 62.

25. *Savannah Morning News*, Oct. 5, 1875.

26. Jones, *Historical Sketch of Tomochichi*, 36.

27. Philip Thickness, *A Year's Journey through France and Part of Spain* (London: 1789), I: 36–37.

28. Ettinger, *James Edward Oglethorpe*, 146, Note 5.

29. Candler, *Colonial Records of Georgia*, II: 123.

30. *Ibid.*, I: 184; Stevens, *History of Georgia*, I: 121.

31. *Journal of the Earl of Egmont*, p. 68.

32. Jones, *History of Georgia*, 183.

33. Bernice McCullar, *This Is Your Georgia* (Montgomery: 1966), p. 121.

34. Candler, *Colonial Records of Georgia*, XX: 246.

35. *Ibid.*, I: 192; III: 93; XX: 246–247; *Journal of the Earl of Egmont*, 156.

36. Candler, *Colonial Records of Georgia*, III: 130.

Chapter 6

THE INDIAN PRINCESS

1. Ellis Merton Coulter, "Mary Musgrove, Queen of the Creeks; a Chapter of Early Georgia Troubles," *Georgia Historical*

Quarterly XI (1): 1–30, March 1927 (Athens: 1927), p. 2.

2. William Bacon Stevens, *History of Georgia* (Savannah: 1972), I: 227.

3. David Corkran, *The Creek Frontier 1540–1783* (Norman: 1967), p. 63.

4. Robert G. McPherson, ed., *Journal of the Earl of Egmont* (Athens: 1962), p. 308.

5. Stevens, *History of Georgia*, I: 229.

6. Sarah B. Gober Temple and Kenneth Coleman, *Georgia Journeys*, Athens: 1961), 82-88; Corkran, *The Creek Frontier*, 90.

7. Latter citation, 90.

8. Albert Samuel Gatschet, *A Migration Legend of the Creek Indians* (AMS Press: 1884–1888), Pt. 2: 235; "Some Ancient Georgia Indian Lore," *Georgia Historical Quarterly* Notes & Documents 15 (2): 192-201, June 1931 (Athens: 1931), 192-198; John Reed Swanton, *Social Organization and Social Usages of the Indians of the Creek Confederacy* (Washington: 1924–25), 34-38. *See also* p. 83, Note 9.

9. "Some Ancient Georgia Indian Lore," 192-201.

10. Georgia Historical Society, *Collections, 1840-1916* (Savannah: 1952-1976), I: 121.

11. *Journal of the Earl of Egmont*, 109.

12. Allen Daniel Candler, *The Colonial Records of the State of Georgia* (Atlanta: 1904–16), XX: 518.

13. Stevens, *History of Georgia*, I: 230.

14. *Idem.*

15. Candler, *Colonial Records*, XX: 247.

16. *Ibid.*, IV: 49-50.

17. *Ibid.*, XXI: 71.

18. Coulter, "Mary Musgrove," 30.

Chapter 7

JOHN WESLEY

1. Robert G. McPherson, ed., *Journal of the Earl of Egmont* (Athens: 1962), p. 120.

2. Allen Daniel Candler, *The Colonial Records of the State of Georgia* (Atlanta: 1904–16), II: 123.

3. *Journal of the Earl of Egmont*, 124.

4. Willie Snow Ethridge, *Strange Fires; the True Story of John Wesley's Love Affair in Georgia* (New York: 1971), 52.

5. *Journal of the Earl of Egmont*, 132.

6. *Ibid.*, 132.

7. Charles Colcock Jones, Jr., *History of Georgia* (Boston: 1883), I: 281.

8. Georgia Historical Society, *Collections 1840–1916* (Savannah: 1952–1976), IV: 51.

9. Thomas Mayhew Cunningham, "Georgia Before Plymouth Rock and Afterwards," *Georgia Historical Quarterly* 33 (3): 206–217, September 1949 (Athens: 1949), 210.

10. Ellis Merton Coulter, "When John Wesley Preached in Georgia," *Georgia Historical Quarterly* 9 (4): 317–351, Dec. 1925 (Athens: 1925), 332.

11. William Bacon Stevens, *History of Georgia* (Savannah: 1972), I: 323.

12. Jones, *History of Georgia*, 281.

13. Leslie Frederic Church, *Knight of the Burning Heart; the Story of John Wesley* (Abingdon: n.d.), 61; Elizabeth Ann Ford, *Jeykl Island* (Savannah: n.d.), 23.

14. David Corkran, *The Creek Frontier 1540–1783* (Norman: 1967), 97.

15. John Wesley, *Journal of the Rev. John Wesley* (London: 1938), I: 239.

16. Charles Colcock Jones, Jr., *Historical Sketch of Tomochichi* (Albany: 1868), 105–106.

17. Stevens, *History of Georgia*, I: 338–339.

18. Sarah B. Gober Temple and Kenneth Coleman, *Georgia Journeys* (Athens: 1961), 89.

19. Wesley, *Journal*, I: 409.

20. Cliff Sewell, *Savannah Now and Then* (Savannah: 1974), 47.

21. Wesley, *Journal*, I: 396, 399.

22. Candler, *Colonial Records of Georgia*, IV: 42.

Chapter 8

THE INDIAN SCHOOL

1. Delores Floyd, *New Yamacraw and the Indian Mound Irene* (Published privately: 1936), 4.

2. Allen Daniel Candler, *The Colonial Records of the State of Georgia* (Atlanta: 1904–16), XX: 247.

3. Delores Floyd, "Yamacraw Queen Senauki," *Savannah Morning News*, May 2, 1937; also in Thomas Gamble Collection, "Georgia Miscellany," XI: 88–91, at Savannah Public Library.

4. Adelaide L. Fries, *The Moravians in Georgia 1735-1740* (Raleigh: 1905), 86.

5. Candler, *Colonial Records*, XXI, 223.

6. W. L. Saunders, ed., *Colonial Records of North Carolina* (Raleigh: 1886–1890), V: 114.

7. Joseph Caldwell, *Irene Mound Site* (Athens: 1941).

The Works Progress Administration under the sponsorship of the Chatham County Commission and the Savannah Chamber of Commerce made an archaeological study of the Irene Mound between 1937 and 1940. A report was published on the investigations. The large mound consisted of eight superimposed rounds, several of which had well-defined occupation levels on the summits and must have been a political center. The smaller mound was the burial place. Much pottery and many skeletons were uncovered. It was thought that Irene was occupied for a considerable time after 1492 and probably almost until the Spanish consolidation of the area about 1600. Since Irene lay on the border between the slightly later Spanish province of Guale and Santa Eleana, there is a fair chance that the inhabitants were Gualean (Yamasee) or Cussabo. They probably spoke a Muskhogean language. They were an educated people who had been in the coastal vicinity for some time. The excavations in 1937 unearthed the cellar of the Indian school. Near this site was the New Yamacraw Indian Village.

8. Candler, *Colonial Records*, XXI: 222.

9. Floyd, "Yamacraw Queen Senauki," p. 90; Thomas Gemble Collection, XI.

10. Candler, *Colonial Records*, XXX: 222.

11. Robert G. McPherson, ed., *Journal of the Earl of Egmont* (Athens: 1962), 291–292.

12. William Bacon Stevens, *History of Georgia* (Savannah: 1972), 366.

Chapter 9

THE SPANISH THREAT

1. Allen Daniel Candler, *The Colonial Records of the State of Georgia* (Atlanta: 1904-16), XX: 544.

2. *Ibid.*, XX: 432.

3. *Ibid.*, XX: 523.

4. Mills Lane, ed., *General Oglethorpe's Georgia; Colonial Letters, 1733–43* (Savannah: 1975), I: 237.

5. Charles Colcock Jones, Jr., *Historical Sketch of Tomochichi* (Albany: 1868), 83–84.

6. Robert G. McPherson, ed., *Journal of the Earl of Egmont* (Athens: 1962), 262.

7. Caroline Couper Lovell, *The Golden Isles of Georgia* (Boston: 1933; Atlanta: 1970), 36.

8. Amos A. Ettinger, *James Edward Oglethorpe* (Oxford: 1936), 252.

9. William Bacon Stevens, *History of Georgia* (Savannah: 1972), I: 151–152; Earl of Egmont, *Diary* (London: 1923), II, 368; 412; Ettinger, *James Edward Oglethorpe*, 19.

> JAMES OGLETHORPE — Captain — 1714, Colonel—August 25, 1737, Brigadier General-1744, Lieutenant General-October 10, 1747, General-February 22, 2765, General of the forces in South Carolina and Georgia-June 1737, Colonel of a regiment to be raised for the defense of Georgia-Sept. 1737.

10. Jones, *Historical Sketch of Tomochichi*, 114.

11. David Corkran, *The Creek Frontier 1540–1783* (Norman: 1967), 100.

12. Charles Colcock Jones, Jr., *History of Georgia* (Boston: 1883), 344.

13. William Bacon Stevens, *History of Georgia* (Savannah: 1972), 158.

Chapter 10

DEATH OF TOMOCHICHI

1. Allen Daniel Candler, *The Colonial Records of the State of Georgia* (Atlanta: 1904-16), IV, 428; William Stephens, *Journal* (Athens: 1949), II: 150; Charles Colcock Jones, Jr., *History of Georgia* (Boston: 1883), I: 320; Charles Colcock Jones, Jr., *Historical Sketch of Tomochichi* (Albany: 1868), 121-122. There is disagreement as to Tomochichi's age at death. Frederick Webb Hodge, *Handbook of American Indians North of Mexico* (Washington: 1907-10), II: 776: "Tomochichi died being perhaps 75 years of age." David Corkran, *The Creek Frontier 1540-1783* (Norman: 1967), 102: "Tomochichi said to be 97 years old at death. Too active to be that old. More likely considerably under 77." Jones, *Historical Sketch of Tomochichi,* 120: "97 years old." *Savannah Georgian,* May 2, 1828: "Tomochichi died at age 97." Albert Samuel Gatschet, *A Migration Legend,* 66: "Tomochichi died about 97 in 1739." Candler, *Colonial Records,* IV: 428: "Death of Tomochichi upward to 90 years." *Dictionary of American Biography,* IX: Pt. 2, 580 — Gives Tomochichi dates 1650?—Oct. 5, 1739. Jones, *History of Georgia,* 320: "Tomochichi died being aged 97."

2. Charles Colcock Jones, Jr., *Antiquities of the Southern Indians* (New York: 1873), 69.

3. Joseph Belcher, *George Whitefield* (New York: n.d.), 60-61.

4. Jones, *Historical Sketch of Tomochichi,* 121.

5. *Gentleman's Magazine* (London: 1740) X: 129; Stephens, *Journal,* II: 153.

6. Candler, *Colonial Records*, V: 323.

7. "Did Tomochichi have trombone music at his funeral?" *Savannah News Press*, Feb. 2, 1958: "Tomochichi may very well have been the first Indian to have trombone music at his funeral. Old Moravian records show that Oglethorpe asked the Moravians to furnish trombone music at the funeral. A little after when the Moravians left for Pennsylvania, Mr. Oglethorpe bought their trumpets and French horns, paying them 10 shillings more than they asked. We must assume the trombones went along with the Moravians." Adelaide L. Fries, *The Moravians in Georgia 1735–1740* (Raleigh: 1905), 214: "The Moravians were asked to furnish music at the funeral but declined." Adelaide L. Fries, ed., *Records of the Moravians in North Carolina* (Raleigh: 1926), III: 1437: "The Moravians who were in Savannah, Georgia, from 1735 to 1740 had trombones and French horns, and they were asked to play for the burial of Tomochichi, the Indian Chief, it is possible that they had been using the instruments in connection with funeral services of their own members, though the Diary of the Georgia Colony of Moravians only says they refused the request for the Tomochichi burial without stating why they were asked, or what use they had been making of the horns."

8. Jones, *Historical Sketch of Tomochichi*, 121–122; *Savannah Morning News*, Nov. 3, 1882.

9. Jones, *History of Georgia*, I: 136.

10. William Bacon Stevens, *History of Georgia* (Savannah: 1972), 158.

Chapter 11

EPILOGUE

1. David Corkran, *The Creek Frontier 1540–1783* (Norman: 1967), 109–110.

2. James Chapman Milling, *Red Carolinians* (Chapel Hill: 1940), 164. John Reed Swanton, *Early History of the Creek Indians and Their Neighbors* (Washington: 1922), 109.

3. *Savannah Morning News*, Sept. 3, 1880.

4. *Ibid.*, Feb. 15, 1878.

5. *Ibid.*, Feb. 14 and 21, 1937.

6. Allen Daniel Candler, *The Colonial Records of the State of Georgia* (Atlanta: 1904-16), VII: 108; VIII: 136, 373.

7. *Savannah Morning News*, Feb. 15, 1878.

8. Candler, *Colonial Records*, VIII: 135-36.

9. *Savannah Morning News*, Feb. 14 and 21, 1937, Nov. 3, 1882; Candler, *Colonial Records*, IV: 603-604; J. W. Hill, *Pictorial View of Savannah 1855*, Lithographed by Charles Parsons.

10. *Savannah Morning News*, Aug. 12, 1962, Magazine Section; Lillian Bragg, "A Dollar for a Monument," *Savannah Morning News*, April 28, 1899; Walter Glasco Charlton, "Dedication of the Memorial to Tomochichi" (in Tomochichi Folder, Reference Department, Savannah Public Library).

BIBLIOGRAPHY

Adair, James, *History of the American Indians*, London: 1775, edited by Samuel Cole Williams. Johnson City, Tennessee: Watauga Press, 1930.

Anderson, Jefferson Randolph, "Genesis of Georgia," *Georgia Historical Quarterly* 13 (3): 231–83, September 1929.

Bakeless, Katherine, *They Saw America First*. New York: Lippincott, 1957.

Bartram, William, *Observations on the Creek and Cherokee Indians*. Transactions, American Ethnological Society III (1). New York: 1853. Reprint 1909.

Belcher, Joseph, *George Whitefield; A Biography with Special Reference to His Labors in America*. New York: American Tract Society, n.d.

Blackburn, Joyce, *James Edward Oglethorpe*. Philadelphia: Lippincott, 1970.

Bourne, Edward, ed., *Narratives of the Career of Hernando de Soto as Told by the Knight of Elvas*. New York: Allerton, 1922. 2 vols.

Brown, Ira L., *The Georgia Colony*. New York: Crowell-Collier, 1970.

Bruce, Henry, *Life of General Oglethorpe*, New York: Dodd, 1890.

Bushnell, David, *Native Villages and Village Sites East of the Mississippi*. Bureau of American Ethnology, Smithsonian Institution Bulletin 69. Washington: Government Printing Office, 1919.

Caldwell, Joseph, and Catherine McCann, *Irene Mound Site*. Athens: University of Georgia Press, 1941.

Callaway, James Etheridge, *The Early Settlement of Georgia*. Athens: University of Georgia Press, 1948.

Candler, Allen D., and Lucian Lamar Knight, eds., *The Colonial Records of the State of Georgia*. 2 vols. Atlanta: Various printers, 1904–1916.

Capps, Clifford Sheats, and Eugenia Burney, *Colonial Georgia*. Nashville: Nelson, 1972.

Church, Leslie Frederic, *Knight of the Burning Heart; the Story of John Wesley*. Abingdon: Cokesbury Press, n.d.

Church, Leslie Frederic, *Oglethorpe*. London: Epworth Press, 1932.

Coleman, Kenneth, and Sarah B. Gober Temple, *Georgia Journeys 1732–54*. Athens: University of Georgia Press, 1961.

Cooper, Walter Gerald, *The Story of Georgia*. New York: American Historical Society, 1938. 3 volumes.

Corkran, David H., *The Creek Frontier 1540-1783*. Norman: University of Oklahoma Press, 1967.

Corry, John Pitts, *Indian Affairs in Georgia, 1732-56*. Philadelphia: Privately printed, 1936.

Coulter, Ellis Merton, "Mary Musgrove, Queen of the Creeks: A Chapter of Early Georgia Troubles," *Georgia Historical Quarterly*, XI (1): 1-30, March 1927.

Coulter, Ellis Merton, "When John Wesley Preached in Georgia," *Georgia Historical Quarterly* 9 (4): 317-351, December 1925.

Crane, Verner Winslow, *The Southern Frontier 1670-1732*. Ann Arbor: University of Michigan, 1929.

Cunningham, Thomas Mayhew, "Georgia—Before Plymouth Rock and Afterwards," *Georgia Historical Quarterly*, 33 (3): 206-217, September 1949.

De Brahm, John Gerar William, *History of the Province of Georgia*. Wormsloe, Georgia: 1849.

DeVorsey, Louis, Jr., "Indian Boundaries in Colonial Georgia," *Georgia Historical Quarterly*, LIV, Spring 1970, 63-78.

Dictionary of American Biography. New York: Scribners, 1936. 11 volumes.

Easterby, J. H., ed., *The Colonial Records of South Carolina*. Columbia: South Carolina Archives Department, 1951—to date. 10 volumes.

Egmont, John Perceval, Earl of, *Diary*. London: H.M. Stationery Office, 1920-1923. 3 volumes.

Egmont, John Perceval, *The Journal of the Earl of Egmont; Abstract of Trustees Proceedings for Establishing the Colony of Georgia 1732-38.* Edited and with an introduction by Robert McPherson. Athens: University of Georgia Press, 1962.

Estill, Eugenia, *James Oglethorpe in England and Georgia.* Charleston: Southern Printing & Publishing Co., 1926.

Ethridge, Willie Snow, *Strange Fires; the True Story of John Wesley's Love Affair in Georgia.* New York: Vanguard Press, 1971.

Ettinger, Amos A., *James Edward Oglethorpe, Imperial Idealist.* Oxford: Clarendon Press, 1936.

Evans, Lawton Bryan, *All About Georgia; Two Hundred Years of Romance and Reality.* New York: American Book Co., 1933.

Evans, Lawton Bryan, *First Lessons in Georgia History.* New York: American Book Company, 1929.

Fancher, Betsy, *The Lost Legacy of Georgia's Golden Isles.* New York: Doubleday, 1971.

Faut, H. B., "The Indian Trade Policy of the Trustees for Establishing the Colony of Georgia in America," *Georgia Historical Quarterly* 15 (3): 207-222, September 1931.

Fitch, Captain, *Journal to the Creeks 1725* (in Mereness, *Newton Dennison Travels in the American Colonies*, 172-212).

Floyd, Delores Boisfeuillet, "Legend of Sir Walter Raleigh at Savannah," *Georgia Historical Quarterly* 23 (2): 103-121, June 1939.

Floyd, Delores Boisfeuillet, *New Yamacraw and the Indian Mound Irene.* Copyright by author: 1936.

Floyd, Delores Boisfeuillet, "Yamacraw Queen Senauki" *Savannah Morning News*, May 2, 1937; Gamble, Thomas, "Georgia Miscellany," XI, 88-91).

Force, Peter, ed., *Transcripts of Georgia Records: Tracts and other Papers Relating Principally to the Origin, settlement and Progress of the Colonies of North America*. Washington: Peter Force, 1836–46. 4 vols.

Ford, Elizabeth Ann, *Jekyll Island*. Savannah: n.d.

Foreman, Carolyn (Thomas), *Indians Abroad 1493–1938*. Norman: University of Oklahoma, 1943.

Fries, Adelaide L., *The Moravians in Georgia 1735–1740*. Raleigh: Edwards, 1905.

Fries, Adelaide L., ed., *Records of the Moravians in North Carolina*. Raleigh: Broughton, 1926.

Gamble, Thomas, "Colonel William Bull—His Part in the Founding of Savannah," *Georgia Historical Quarterly*, XVII (2): 111–126, June 1933.

Gatschet, Albert Samuel, *A Migration Legend of the Creek Indians*. AMS Press, Inc., 1884–1888. 2 volumes.

Georgia Historical Quarterly 15 (2): 192–201, June 1931: "Notes & Documents, Some Ancient Georgia Indian Lore."

Georgia Historical Society, *Collections*. Savannah: Printed for the Society, 1840–1916.

Gordon, Peter, *The Journal of Peter Gordon*. Edited by E. Merton Coulter. Athens: University of Georgia Press, 1963.

Green, Edwin, *Indians of South Carolina*. Columbia: University of South Carolina Press, 1920.

Harden, William, *A History of Savannah and South Georgia*. Chicago: Lewis, 1913. 2 volumes.

Harris, Thaddeus Mason, *Biographical Memorials of James Oglethorpe*. Boston: Privately printed, 1841.

Harris, Walter A., *Emperor Brim, the Greatest American Indian*. Macon: Burke, 1937.

Harris, Walter A., *Here the Creeks Sat Down*. Macon: Burke, 1958.

Harris, Walter A., "Old Ocmulgee Fields," *Georgia Historical Quarterly*, XIX (4): 273–287, December 1935.

Hodge, Frederick Webb, ed., *Handbook of American Indians North of Mexico*. Bureau of American Ethnology, Smithsonian Institution Bulletin 30. Washington: Government Printing Office, 1907–10. 2 volumes.

Indian Book, *Journal of the Cherokee Trade*. Middle 18th Century, Archives of the South Carolina Historical Association (Schoolcraft), Charleston. 6 volumes.

Ivers, Larry E., *South Carolina 1670–1775*. Tricentennial Booklet No. 3. Charleston: 1975.

Johnson, Amanda, *Georgia as Colony and State*. Atlanta: Brown, 1938.

Johnson, James Guyton, "The Yamassee Revolt of 1597 and the Destruction of the Georgia Missions," *Georgia Historical Quarterly*, 7 (1): 44–53, 1923.

Jones, Charles Colcock, Jr., *Antiquities of the Southern Indians, Particularly of the Georgia Tribes*. New York: Appleton and Company, 1873.

Jones, Charles Colcock, Jr., *Historical Sketch of Tomochichi*. Albany, New York: Munsell, 1868.

Jones, Charles Colcock, Jr., *History of Georgia*. Boston: Houghton-Mifflin. 1883. 2 volumes.

Jones, Charles Colcock, Jr. *History of Savannah, Georgia*. Syracuse: Mason, 1890.

Kroll, Harry Harrison, *The Long Quest; the Story of John Wesley*. Philadelphia: Westminster, 1954.

Lane, Mills, ed., *General Oglethorpe's Georgia; Colonial Letters, 1773–43*. Savannah: Beehive Press, 1975. 2 volumes.

Lanning, John Tate, *Spanish Missions of Georgia*. Chapel Hill: University of North Carolina Press, 1935.

Lovell, Caroline Couper, *The Golden Isles of Georgia*. Boston: Little, Brown, 1933; Atlanta: Cherokee Publishing Company, 1970.

McCall, Hugh, *The History of Georgia*. Atlanta: Seymour Williams, 1909.

McCullar, Bernice, *This is Your Georgia*. Northport: Southern Publishing Co., 1966.

McGrady, Edward, *The History of South Carolina under the Royal Government 1719-1776*. New York: Russell & Russell, 1899.

Martin, Paul Sidney, *Indians before Columbus*. Chicago: University of Chicago Press, 1947.

Mereness, Newton Dennison, *Travels in the American Colonies*. New York: Macmillan Company, 1916.

Mikell, H. J., "Founding of the Church in Georgia," *Georgia Historical Quarterly* XVII (2): 77–90, June 1933.

Milling, Chapman James, *Red Carolinians*. Chapel Hill: University of North Carolina Press, 1940.

Oglethorpe, James, "Letters to the Trustees of the Colony and Others from October 1735 to August 1744," *Georgia Historical Society Collections 1840-1959*, III: 1-156.

Parks, Aileen Wells, *James Oglethorpe, Young Defender*. Indianapolis: Bobbs, Merrill, 1960.

Pickett, Albert James, *History of Alabama and Incidentally of Georgia and Mississippi from the Earliest Period*. Birmingham: By author, 1900. 2 volumes.

Reck, George Philipp von, Baron, "Commissary Von Reck's Report on Georgia," Translated by George Fenwick Jones. *Georgia Historical Quarterly*, 47 (1): 95-100, March 1963.

Reese, Trevor, *Colonial Georgia*. Athens: University of Georgia Press, 1963.

Sass, Herbert Ravenel, *The Story of the South Carolina Low Country*. West Columbia: J.F. Hyer, n.d. 3 volumes.

Saunders, William L., ed., *The Colonial Records of North Carolina*. Raleigh: P.M. Hale, 1886-1890. 10 volumes.

Schoolcraft, Henry R. "Indian Tribes of the U.S." Compiled by Frances Nichols. Bureau of American Ethnology, *Smithsonian Institution Bulletin* 152. Washington: Government Printing Office, 1954.

Sewell, Cliff, *Savannah, Now and Then*. Savannah: Printcraft Press, 1974.

Sherwood, Adiel, *A Gazeteer of the State of Georgia*. Athens: University of Georgia Press, 1939.

Sirmans, M. Eugene, *Colonial South Carolina; a Political History 1663-1763*. Chapel Hill: University of North Carolina, 1966.

Stephens, William, *The Journal of William Stephens*. Edited by E. Merton Coulter. Athens: University of Georgia Press, 1958-1959. 2 volumes.

Stevens, William Bacon, *History of Georgia*. Savannah: Bee Hive Press, 1972. 2 volumes.

Stokes, Thomas L., *The Savannah*. New York: Rinehart & Company, 1951.

Suddeth, Ruth Elgin, *Empire Builders of Georgia*. Austin: Steck Co., 1951.

Swanton, John Reed, "Early History of the Creek Indians and Their Neighbors," Bureau of American Ethnology, *Smithsonian Institution Bulletin* 73. Washington: Government Printing Office, 1922.

Swanton, John Reed, "The Indian Tribes of North America," Bureau of American Ethnology, *Smithsonian Institution Bulletin* 145. Washington: Government Printing Office, 1952.

Swanton, John Reed, "Indians of the Southeastern United States," Bureau of American Ethnology, *Smithsonian Institution Bulletin* 137. Washington: Government Printing Office, 1946.

Swanton, John Reed, "Social Organization and Social Usages of the Indians of the Creek Confederacy," *Bureau of American Ethnology 42nd Annual Report 1924-25*. Washington: Government Printing Office, 1928.

Tailfer, Patrick, "True and Historical Narrative of the Colony in America," *Georgia Historical Society Collections*, II: 165–263.

Thickness, Philip, *A Year's Journey through France and Part of Spain*. 3rd. ed. London: 1789. 2 volumes.

United States De Soto Expedition (De Soto's route). Final report of the U.S. De Soto Expedition Commission. Washington: Government Printing Office, 1939.

Urlsperger, Samuel, ed., *Detailed Reports on the Salzburger Emigrants Who Settled in America*. Edited by George Fenwick Jones; translated by Hermann Lacher. Athens: University of Georgia Press, 1968. 3 volumes.

Vaeth, Joseph Gordon, *The Man Who Founded Georgia*. New York: Crowell-Collier, 1968.

Wesley, John, *Journal of the Reverend John Wesley*. Edited by Nehemiah Curnoch. London: Epworth Press, 1938. 8 volumes.

Whitefield, George, *Journal*. London: James Hutton, 1739–41. 6 volumes.

Wright, Robert, *A Memoir of General James Oglethorpe*. London: Chapman & Hall, 1867.

INDEX

177

CPSIA information can be obtained
at www.ICGtesting.com
Printed in the USA
LVHW111552211218
601372LV00001B/23/P

9 780877 973171